Backyard Pioneers

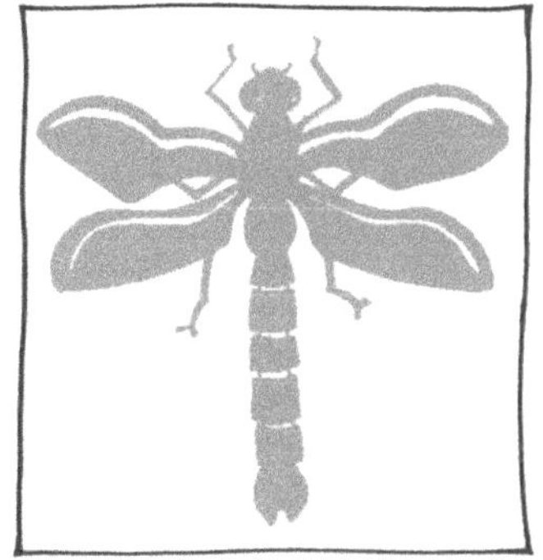
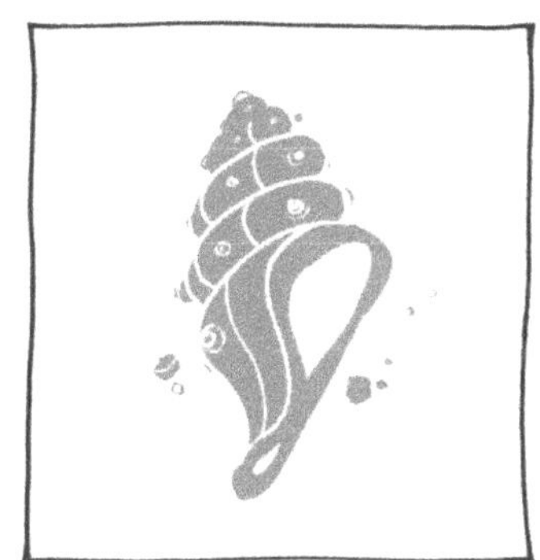
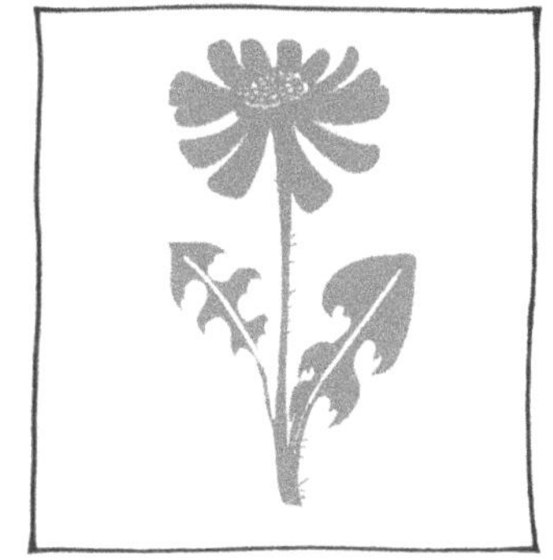
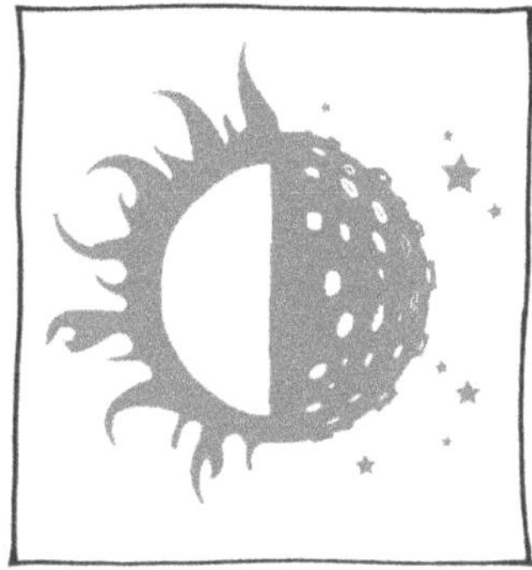

Outdoor Artists

Series Editor & Concept by: Julie Elledge PhD., LMFT, MCC, NBHWC

Illustrated by: Kevin Gleason

Writers: Kevin Gleason & Jackie Gilmore

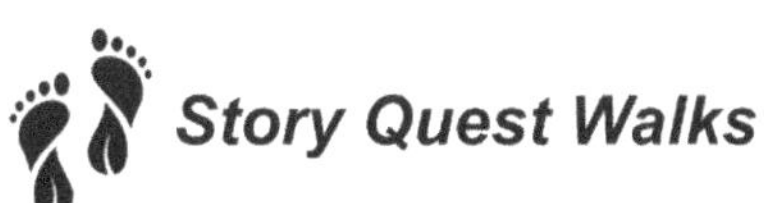 **Story Quest Walks**

BY

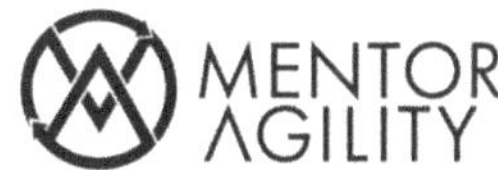
MENTOR AGILITY

Contents

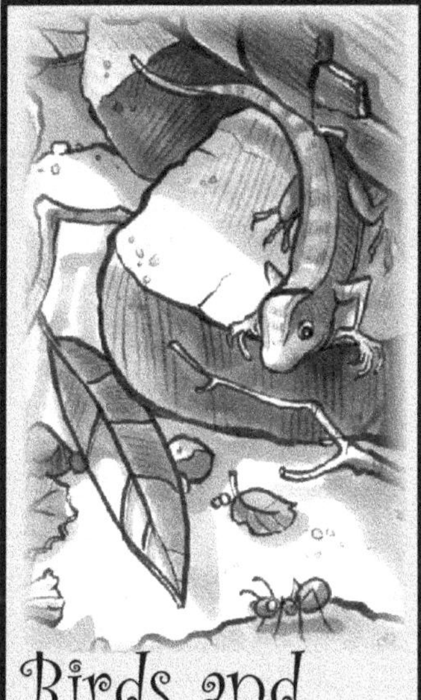

Birds and Insects

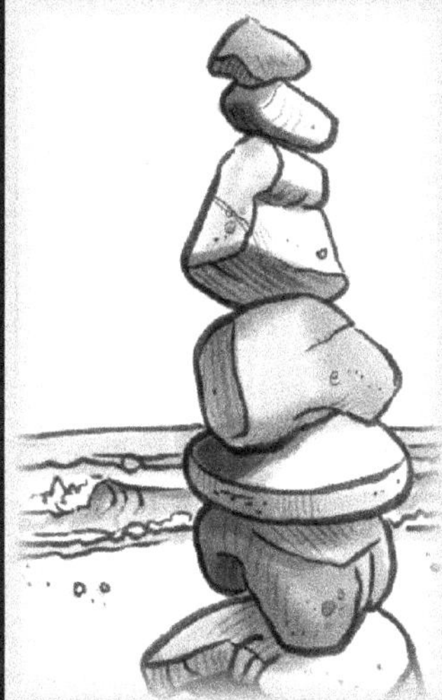

Stones and Structure

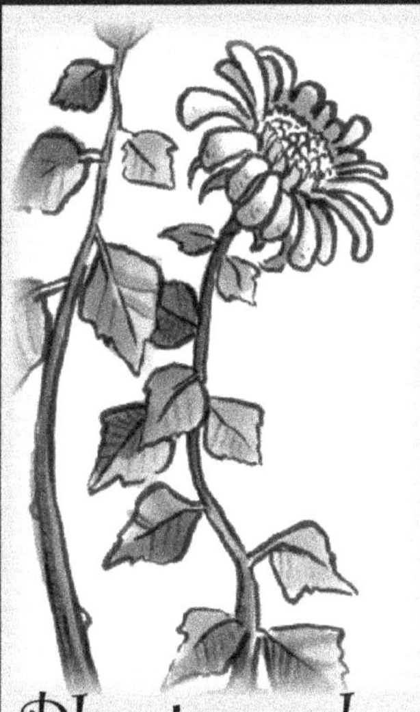

Plants and Flowers

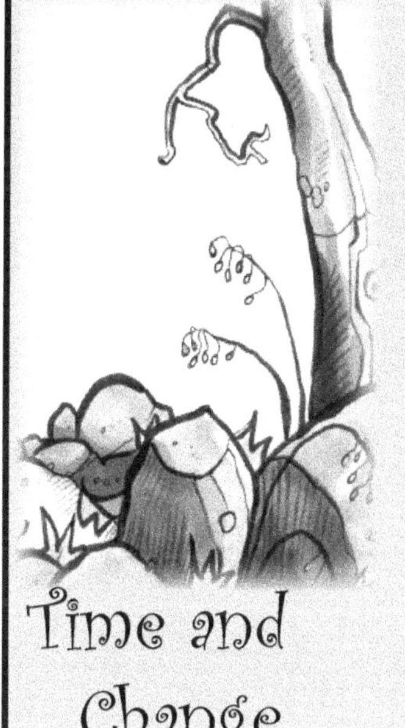

Time and Change

What is that in the top right corner?
(see page 104)

Letter to Parents

Exploring nature helps children become confident, observant, sensitive and compassionate citizens of our planet. They understand from direct experience the connections between all living things and develop a lifelong sense of curiosity and wonder toward the natural world. An understanding of the balance and harmony intrinsic in nature will always comfort them.

Art provides one of the most direct ways of exploring and studying the world. From the time that earliest humans painted upon cave walls, people of all cultures around the globe have felt the need to express themselves and their experience of the natural world. Children who practice art develop essential skills of observation, hand-eye coordination, creativity, craftsmanship and communication. A strong basis in art intensifies all other types of learning.

Pablo Picasso is famous for saying, "All children are artists. The problem is how to remain an artist once we grow up." Set a child loose in a mountain meadow, and you will realize that Picasso's quote may also hold true for "naturalists." As artists, we learn early on to be critical and filter our creativity into the narrow-minded boxes of convention. This is a book to help you and your children look at your backyard wilderness and the experience of making art with innocent eyes, as though seeing and drawing for the first time. This is how we open ourselves up to really learning something new.

In this book, you will discover a wide variety of art experiences. There are interactive art games to play outdoors, step-by-step drawing and shading activities, unusual sculpture opportunities, and fun, unconventional art lessons. They use relatively simple supplies. If you have pencils, paper, scissors, glue and colored pencils, you can do most of the lessons. Throw in watercolors and a bottle of ink, and you can do them all.

The idea is for these to be experiences you share with your children. The artists' biographies and chapter headings are intended to stimulate conversations about art and nature with your children.

Most importantly, this is a book to get you and your kids outside. Our greatest hope is that you will find yourselves resting in the breezy shade peering out over a stunning landscape. With colored pencils or watercolors in hand, we hope you will be out there drawing the bugs and weeds with abandon, leaving a trail of colorful paintings and drawings that will always rekindle memories of your shared adventures and experiences outdoors.

Letter to Students

This is a book for people who love nature and love to create art. Every project in this book will get you and your parents outdoors exploring the world, and then teach you how to create an art project about your experience. You will learn to draw from life, to make sculptures from unusual materials, to make comics and flipbooks, and to see art in entirely new ways.

When you find some free time to start enjoying this book, don't spend too much time indoors reading all the lessons. Just flip through randomly and point to any page. Let that be your adventure for the day and head out the door. You can never get outside too soon.

Before you actually start drawing, make sure you take the time to climb a tree, run up a hill or race a tumbleweed so that you feel ready to sit down and concentrate for a while. If you are losing interest in a drawing, it is always okay to stop for a while, roll down a grassy hill, and come back to finish it the next day. The secret of making thoughtful, beautiful art is this: The more fun you have creating something, the more fun others will have looking at your work.

Don't let your parents be too hard on themselves if their drawings don't look as good as yours. Remind them that the more they practice, the better they'll get. Remind them that the whole point of this is to have fun, to look closely at nature, to get a little bit dirty, and to feel the happiness that comes from making something with your own two hands. Even if their drawings aren't perfect, the memories of the day they spent crawling after you through the bushes are priceless masterpieces.

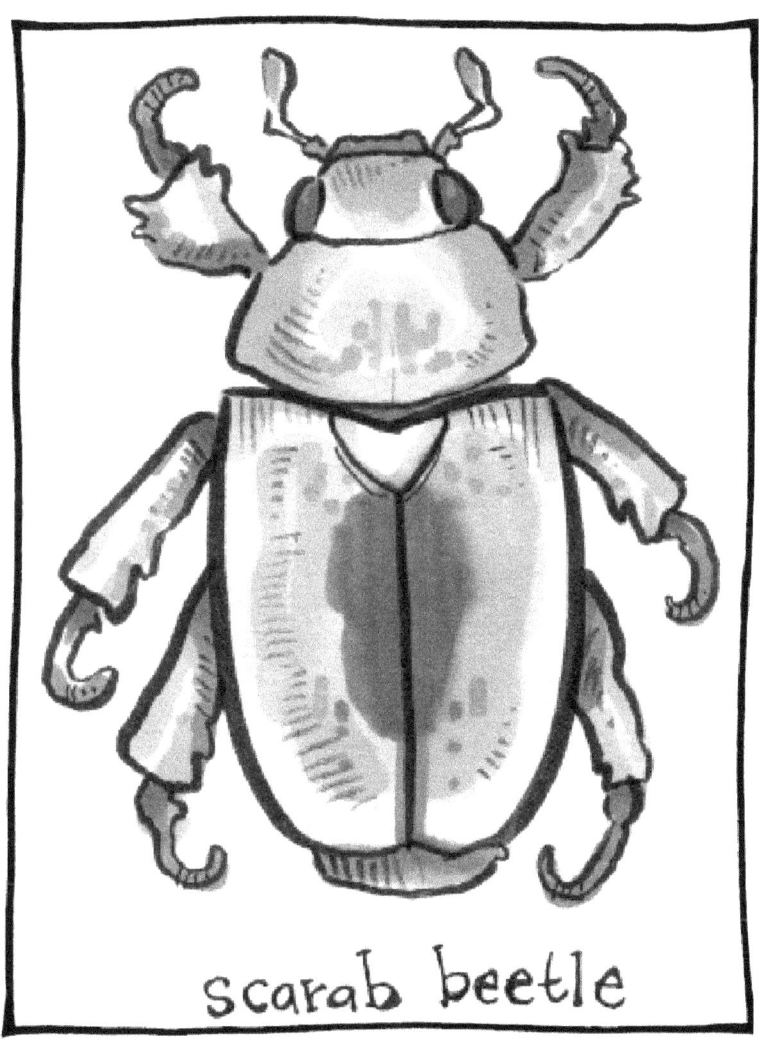

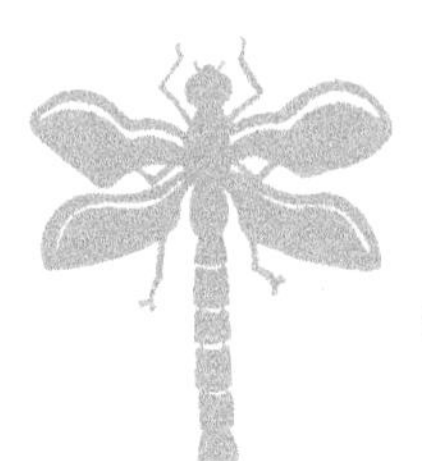

Birds and Insects

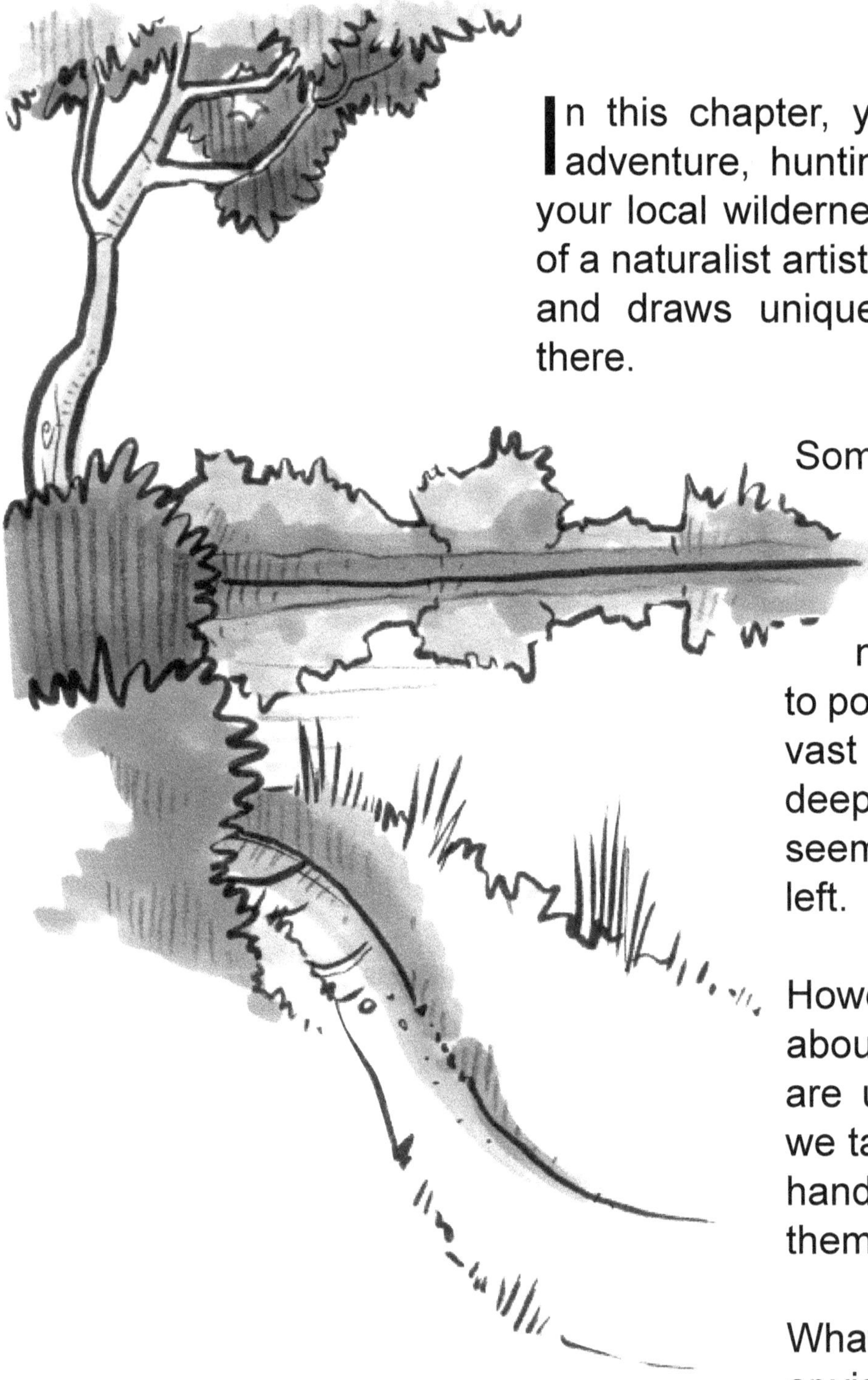

In this chapter, you will go on a backyard adventure, hunting for birds and insects in your local wilderness. You will learn the skills of a naturalist artist who explores new frontiers and draws unique birds and insects living there.

Sometimes it feels like all of earth's frontiers have already been explored. People have stepped nearly everywhere, from pole to pole. They have even crossed vast deserts and jungles. The deepest oceans and outer space seem to be the only frontiers left.

However, when we really think about it, even our own backyards are unexplored wild lands until we take the time to crawl on our hands and knees and rediscover them.

What creatures live in your yard or visit in the middle of the night? What do those creatures like to eat?

What birds visit your neighborhood with the changing seasons? What brings them there?

These are the types of questions that neighborhood naturalists ask as they walk around the block looking in the bushes for birds' nests.

It is fascinating to see what we encounter when we take the time to step off the well-worn trails in our neighborhoods. There are little pockets of wilderness hidden all around us that we pass by every day.

If we think like a naturalist, we can break our routines and peer through fences and behind hedges into vacant places we have overlooked, then draw what we discover.

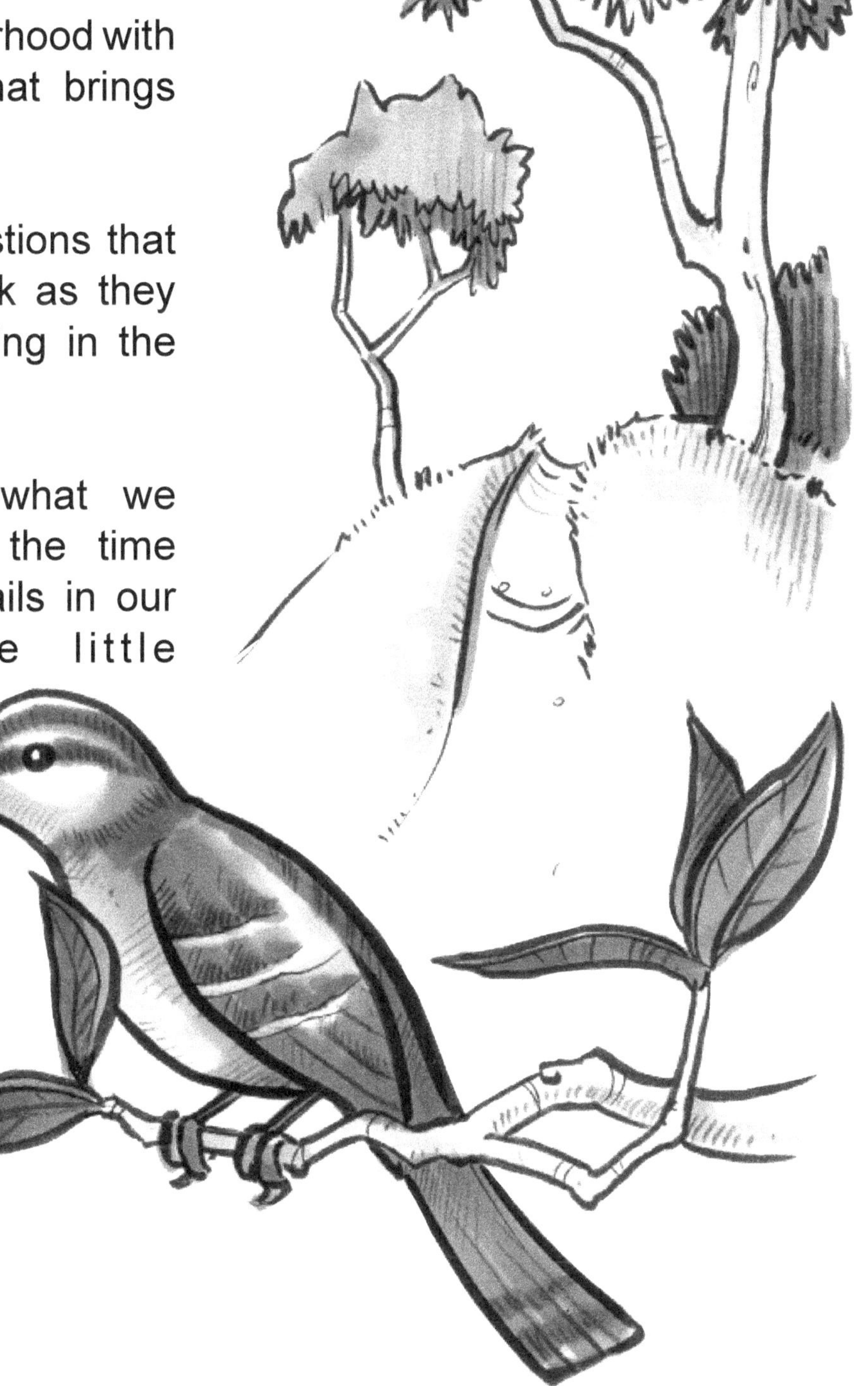

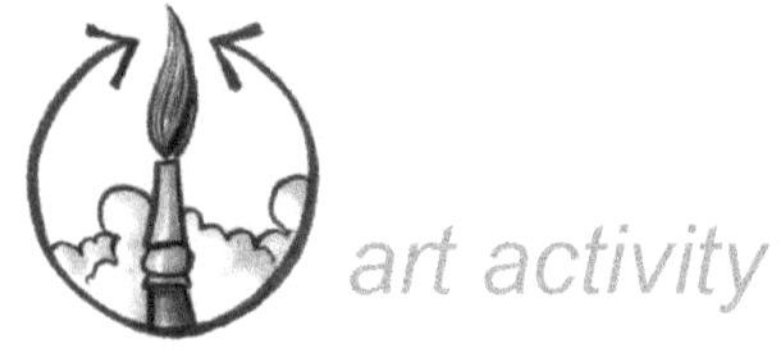

Invent a Bug

Background: Scientists have found and named over one million insect species in the world. This means that there are more insect species than the total of all other species of creatures on the earth. Even more amazing than that, most scientists agree that we have probably discovered less than half of the insects that are actually out there. So, there are plenty of six-legged creatures still crawling around for you to discover and name for yourself.

Think of the forms bugs and insects can take. They are built with wings, enormous jaws, antennae, compound eyes, and often, many legs. Picture the rhinoceros beetle, the praying mantis, the ladybug, the mosquito, and the dragonfly, and you will begin to appreciate the marvelous forms insects can take.

Go outside and turn over some rocks or wood, and search for the most unusual bug you can find. Draw its portrait in the space below.

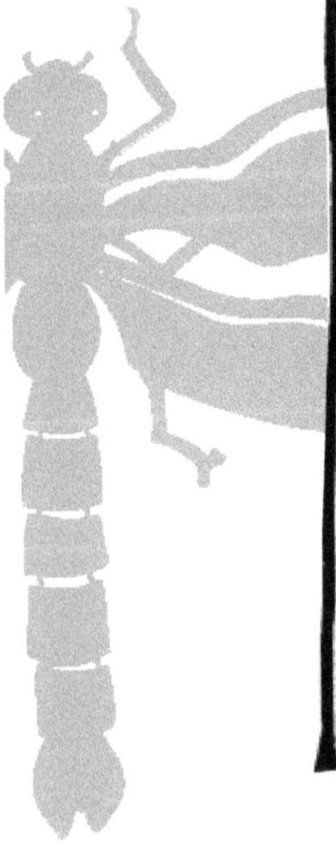

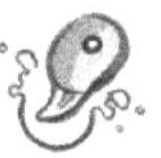

Materials: Any drawing tools will work. Colored pencils and black pens are always a fun option.

Project Description: In this project, you will start with a simple shape and then make it more and more complicated. On the next page, you will create the most unusual, unique bug you can imagine.

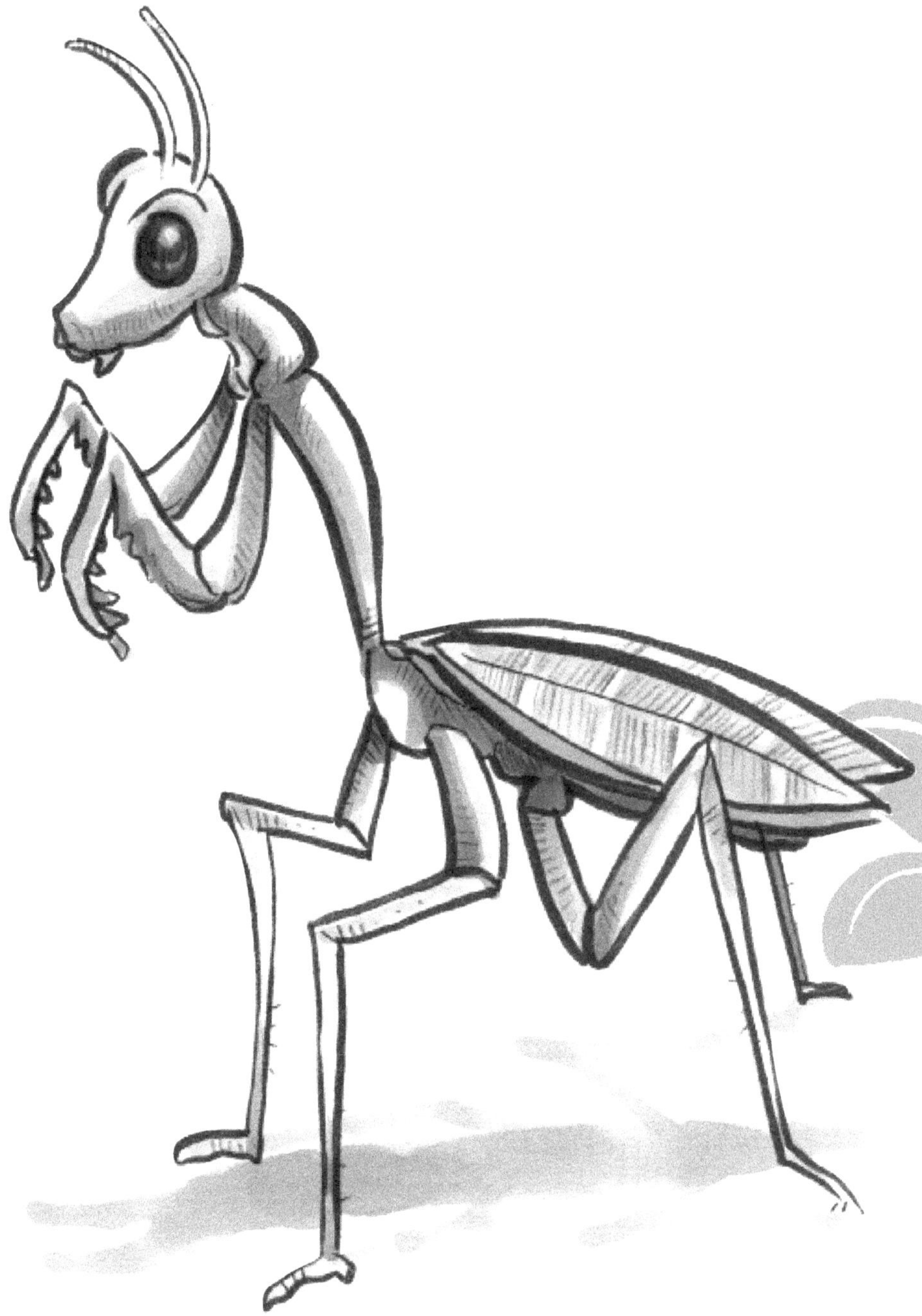

Directions:

- Start by drawing three shapes for your bug's body. These shapes are called the head, thorax and abdomen. You can make them any size and shape you like.

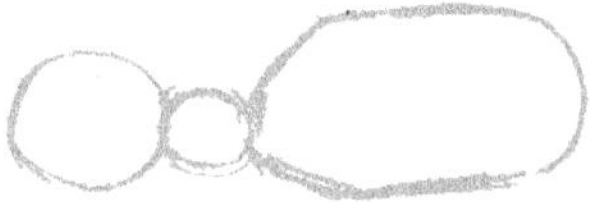

- Now, one by one, start adding body parts to your insect. Maybe you will add six hairy legs, butterfly wings, a scorpion tail, ant jaws, and praying mantis arms. You can add parts nobody has heard of yet that will help your bug do amazing things. Think about how it might move and how it gets its food. Try to fill your drawing with as many details as possible.

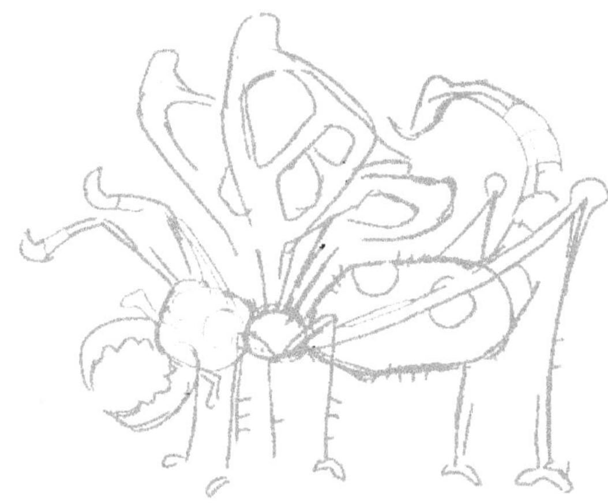

- When you don't think you could add one more part, add one more part. Add color or any other details you can think of.

- Name your bug.

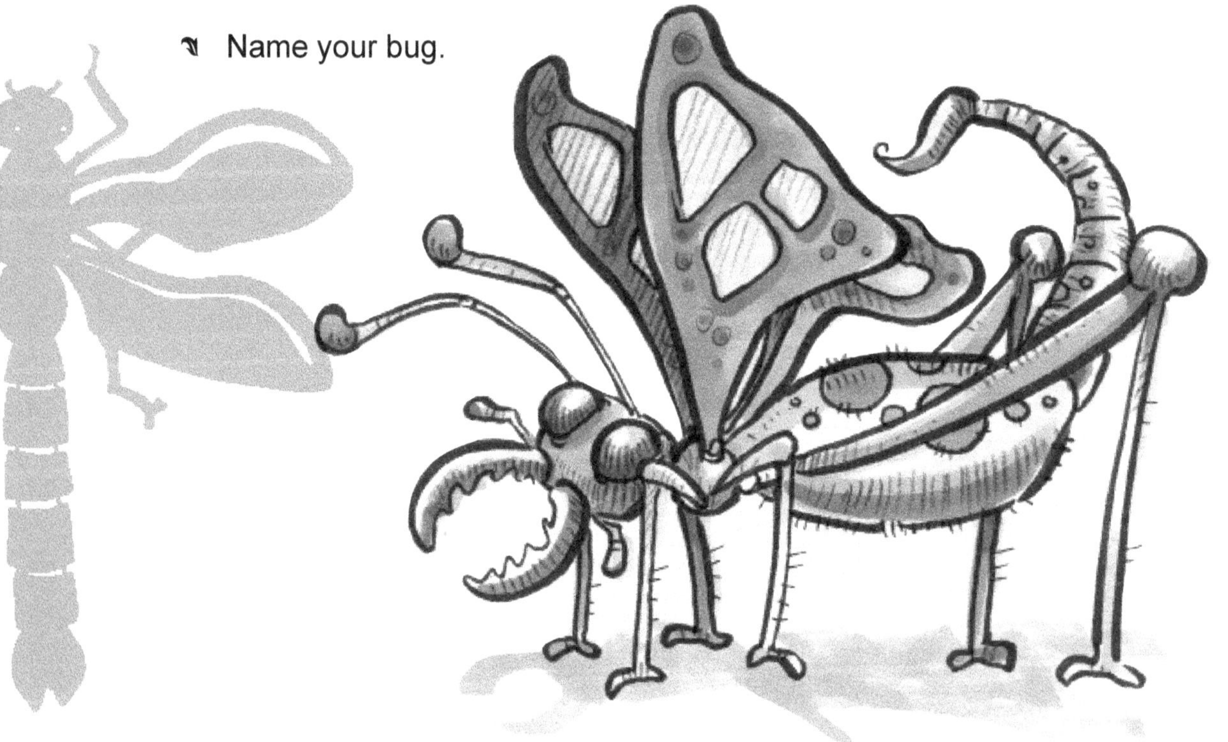

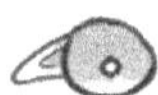

insect name: _______________________________

Consider This: We have two eyes for a reason. Our brain mixes the two views we see together, and this helps us see things in three dimensions so that we can tell how far away things are. Insects often have compound eyes, made up of thousands of lenses. What do you think this helps a bug to see? Many insects can see colors that we can't. Many can see ultraviolet light, which is invisible to our eyes. Some flowers are colored with ultraviolet designs that help insects find them. Make a drawing of how you imagine a flower might look to a bee.

Going Further: Try to build your bug out of modeling clay or other materials you can find around the house. Put it on your parent's pillow, and see if you can scare them.

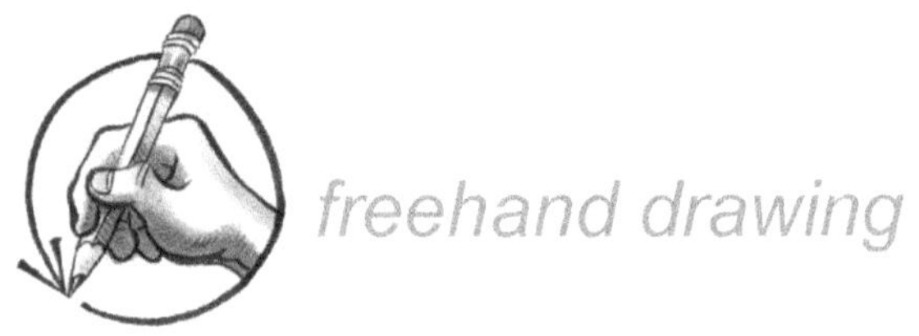

Drawing a Honey Bee Step-By-Step

Background: In this book you will find several step-by-step drawing lessons. When you have the chance, it is always better to draw from real life as opposed to copying other artist's drawings or working from photographs. That way, everything you make will be completely original and from your true experience. But, at times it can be helpful to follow along with another artist and learn how they build images. That way you will know some drawing techniques to help you create your own vision.

Directions: Follow along with these steps in the frame on the next page.

- Do these first steps very lightly with pencil. You will erase some of these lines later, but in the meantime, they will help you develop more complicated forms. Start with a basic head, thorax and abdomen as in the last lesson.

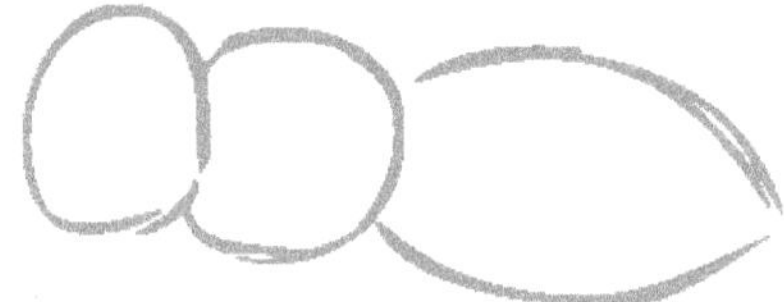

- Add lines to start the legs, wings, antennae and eyes.

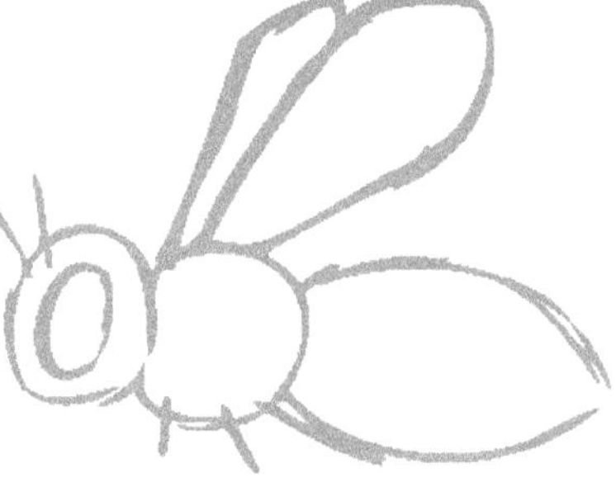

- Extend these lines and add stripes to the body.

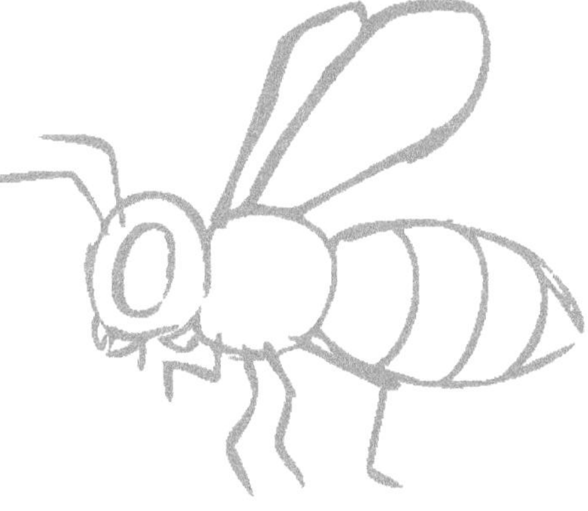

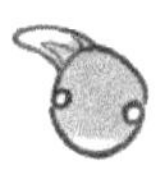

❧ Add more details to the wings and thickness to the legs and stripes.

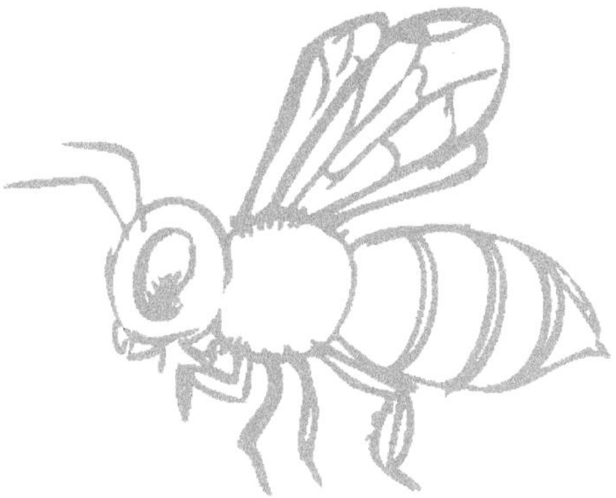

❧ Using your pencil or a black pen, darken your outlines and erase lighter lines.

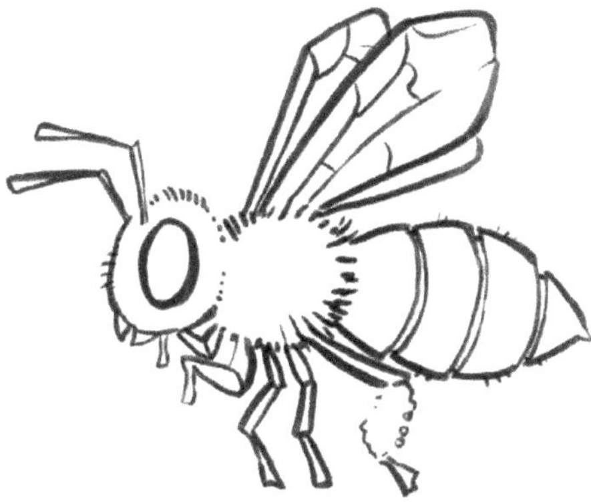

❧ Lightly using your pencil, as shown in the lesson "Learning to Shade Your Drawings" in the next chapter, begin to build up some light grey tones in the areas shown below.

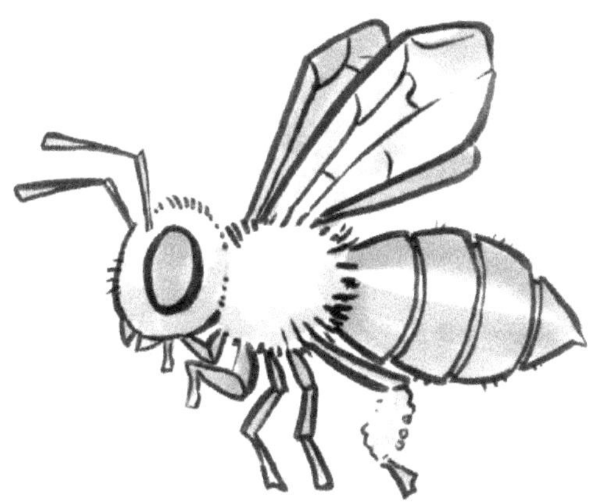

❧ Build up your shadows so you have more shades of grey and black. Add furry textures to the bee's body and with a sharp pencil, add as many details as you can.

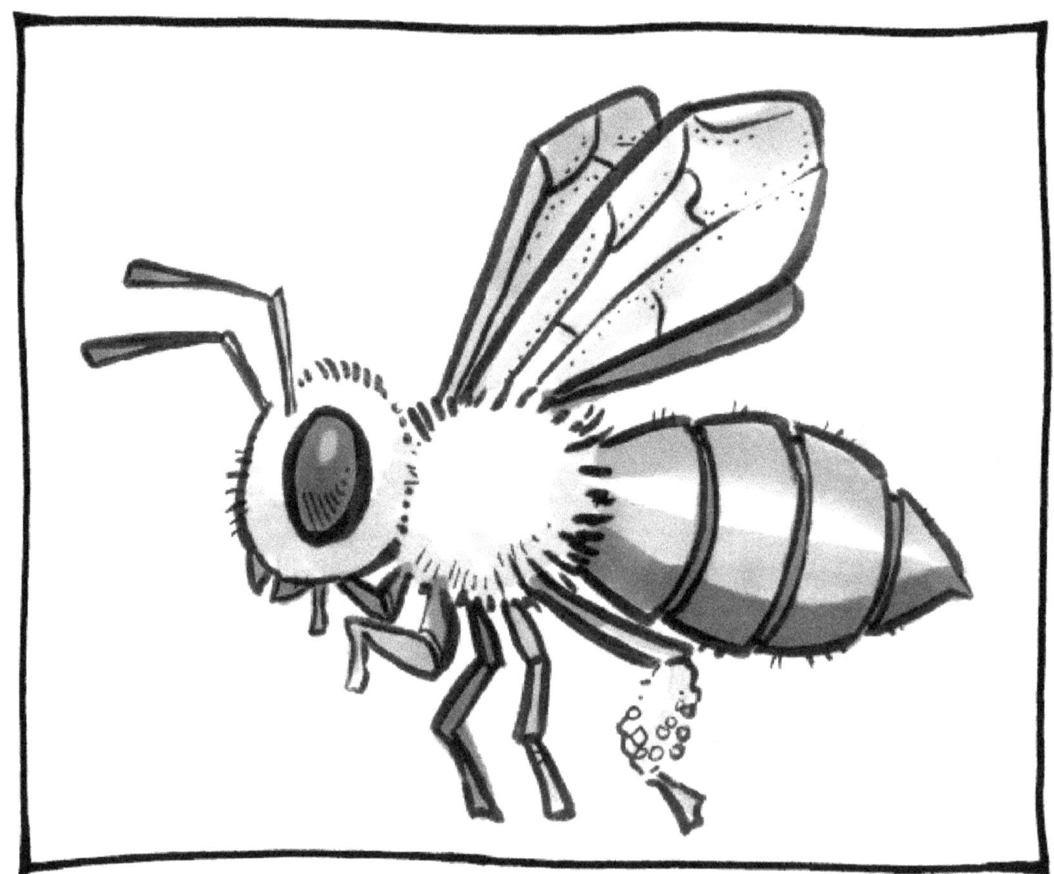

Going Further: You have learned why it is important to draw from real life, but of course it can also be an excellent experience to draw from your imagination. The techniques that you have learned will help you take the pictures that you imagine in your head and bring them to life as well. Try drawing a pet following these same steps. If you don't have a pet, adopt a bug outside and draw it instead.

Turn the book sideways, so you can make your bee nice and large. This will help you to get all of the details. Remember to start off lightly so you can erase lines later.

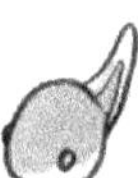

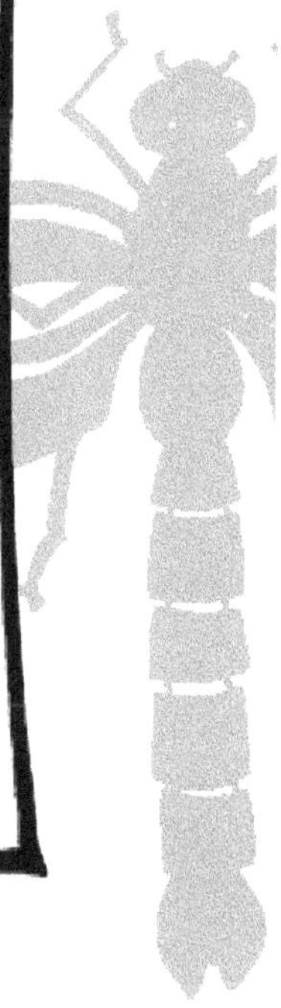

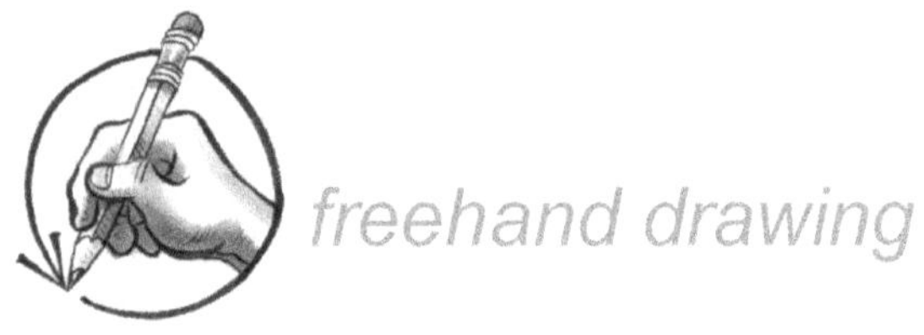

Taking a Line for a Walk

Background: The artist Jasper Johns once said, "Making a drawing is like taking a line for a walk." Imagine your pencil traveling across the page. The pencil's point draws everything you see in the world in front of you. You could also say that making a drawing is like taking your eyes for a walk. They walk through the scene that you are looking at, and your pencil traces their path on your paper.

Project Description: For this project, you will be taking a walk with your eyes through a natural scene while your pencil slowly wanders across your paper recording the trail. This is one of the best activities for teaching your hand and eyes to work together. It helps you slow down and observe the world more closely. If you practice this often, you will notice that your drawing ability will greatly improve. Also, your way of seeing the world will change in subtle, beautiful ways.

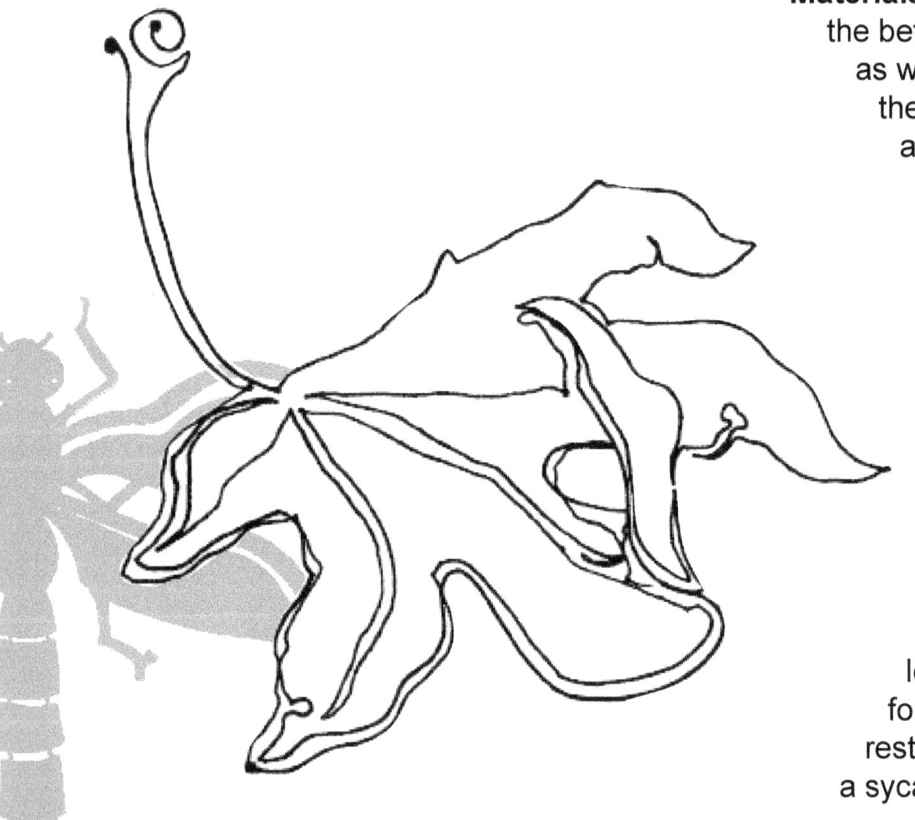

Materials: Pen and paper — the larger the better. You could use a pencil as well, as long as you don't use the eraser. Do not worry about accidents on this drawing.

Directions:

- Find a comfortable place outside to sit and draw.

- Put the point of your pencil in the center of the paper.

- Look out into the landscape and find a place that looks like a good center point for your drawing. Let your eyes rest there for a while. Perhaps it is a sycamore leaf lying on a rock.

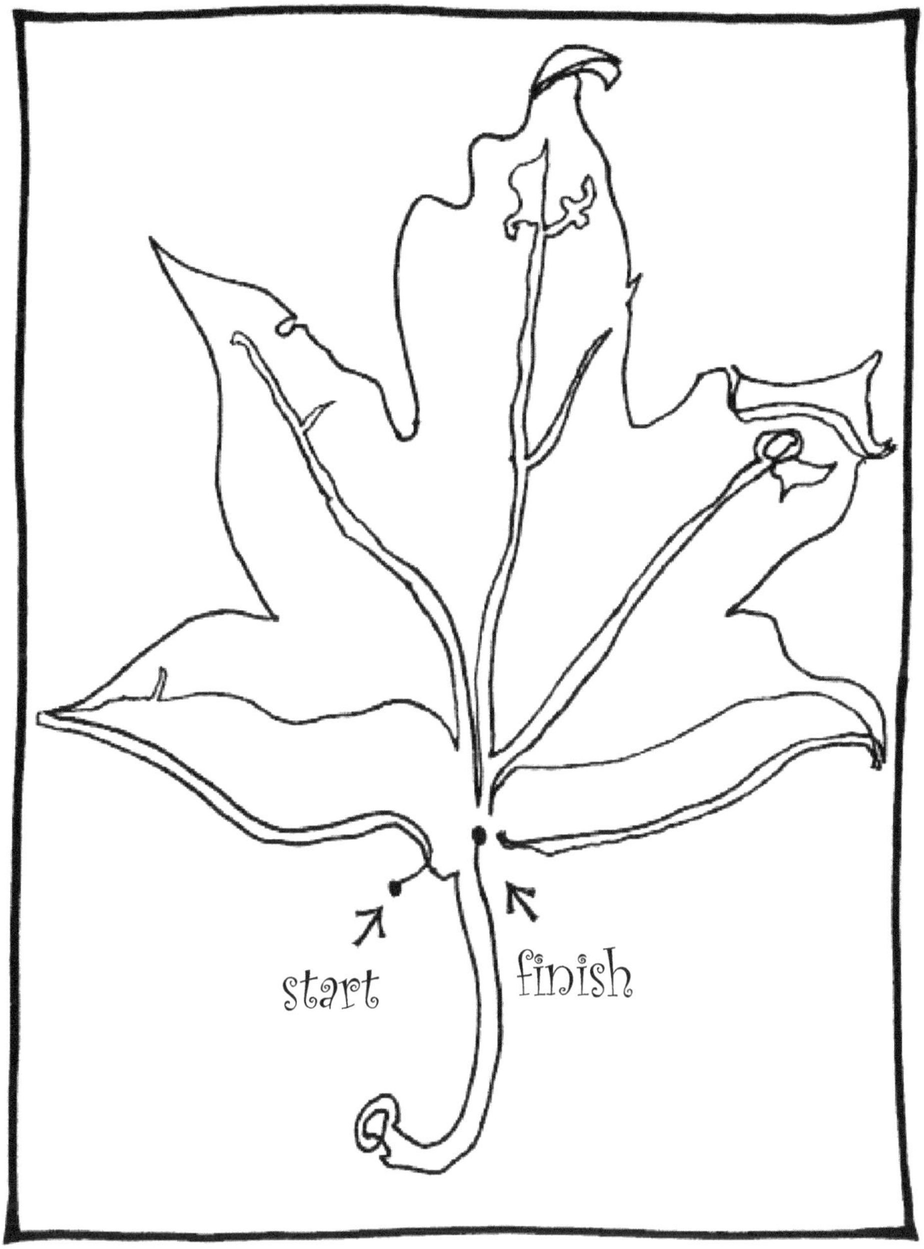

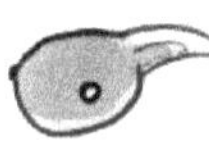

❧ You are going to make a drawing of the scene without ever lifting your pencil. Your eyes are going to travel slowly around the shape of the sycamore leaf, to the rock, and then into the rest of the scene. Your pencil is going to slowly follow the path of your eyes.

❧ You may find it helpful to imagine a small ant sitting on the edge of the leaf, or whatever you are drawing. Imagine the ant walking very slowly along the edges of the leaf. As it walks, your hand slowly moves your pencil along its path. It may walk along the veins of the leaf. It may walk along the edge of the leaf's shadow. Just keep following lines with your eyes and drawing them on your paper. Go as slowly as you can.

❧ If your hand or your eyes try to speed up, stop for a second. Take a breath. Then start again, slowly. Be patient, and take the time to follow all of the little cracks and details in the rock that the leaf is sitting on.

❧ You will want to look down at your paper at times to see your progress and to make sure things are in the right place. This is fine, but always stop drawing to look at your paper. You should only let your pencil move when it is following the path of your eyes.

❧ When you are happy with your drawing, stop. Get up and take a walk with your feet, and when you find another nice place to sit, go for another walk with your eyes and a pencil.

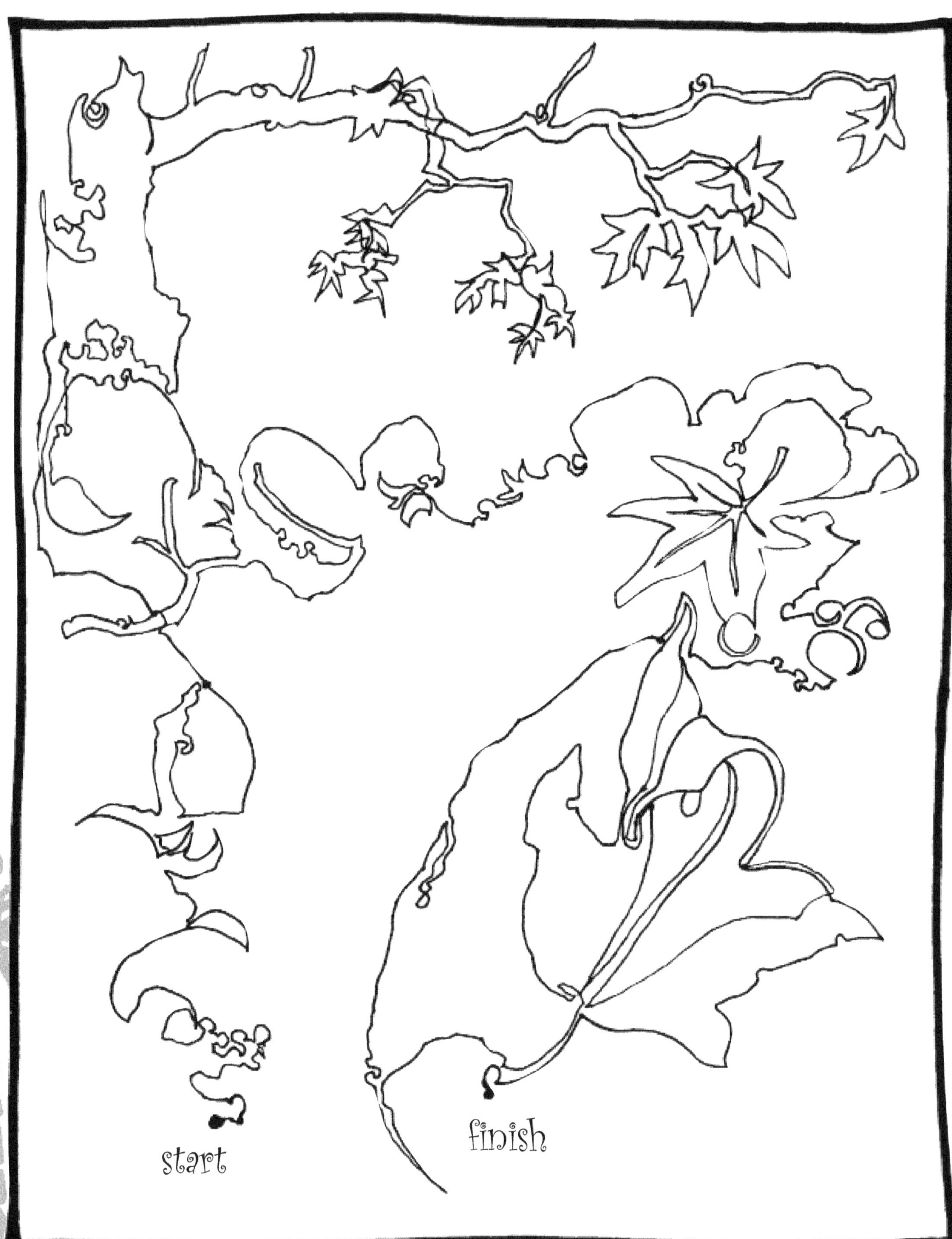

start
finish

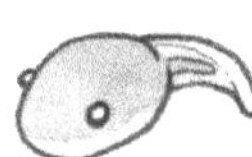

Notice This: You have made a drawing with one long line. This drawing is like a knit sweater: if you pulled the end of it like a thread, you could unravel the whole thing. If your drawing were a plate of spaghetti, you could eat it with one long slurp. What connects all the things in your drawing besides the single line you drew?

____

____

____

____

____

____

Consider This: At first, when people do these types of drawings, they are very tense. It takes a lot of concentration, so they hold their breath and grit their teeth. Notice how the way you feel changes as you do this activity. After a while, we tend to relax, and our experience can be very pleasant. We realize that it is actually quite simple just to sit, feel the breeze, look out at the landscape, and move our pencils across our paper. Many people begin to see things a little differently.

What types of things did you become aware of as you drew?

____

____

____

Do you notice any changes in the way you see your surroundings after doing a drawing like this?

____

____

____

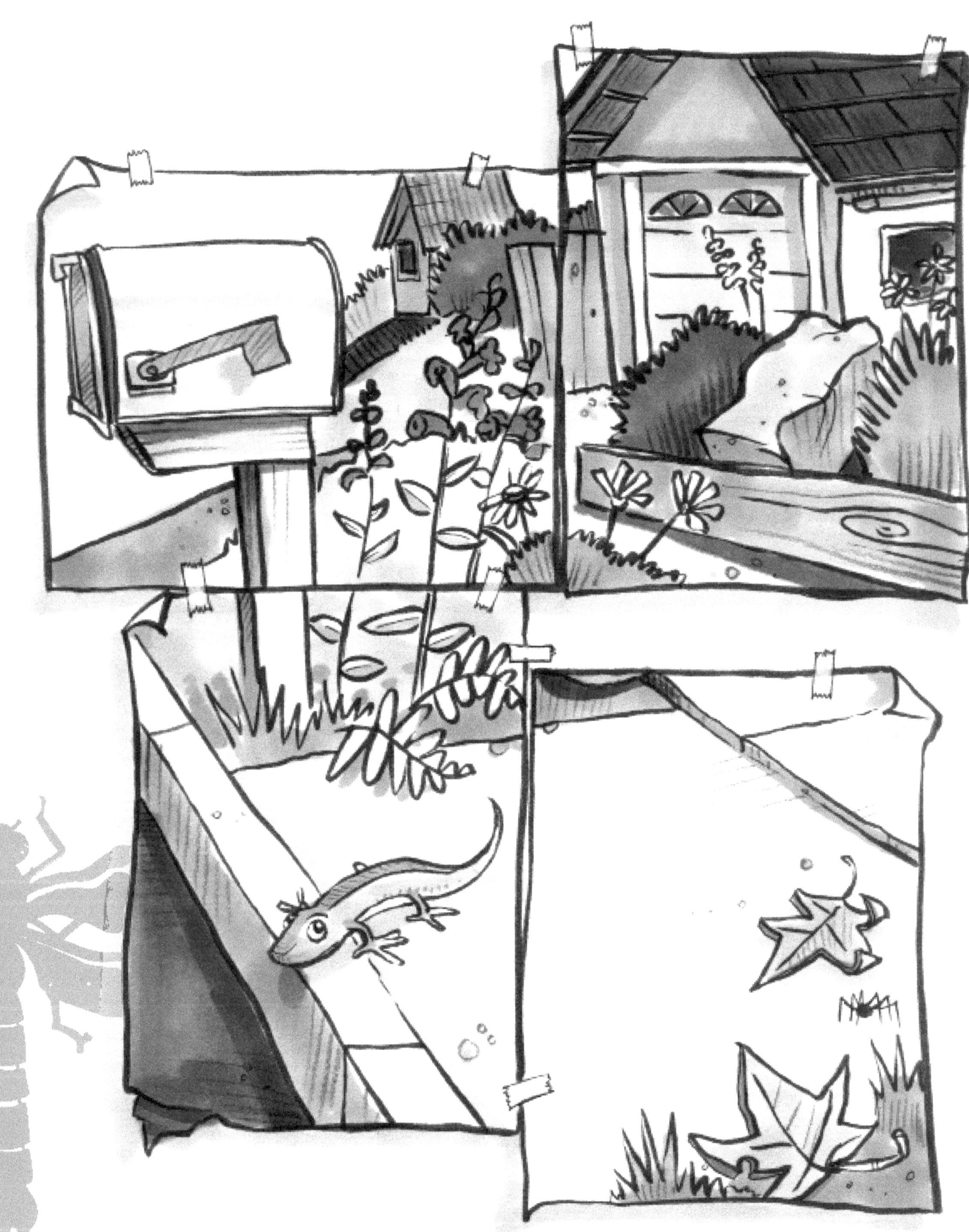

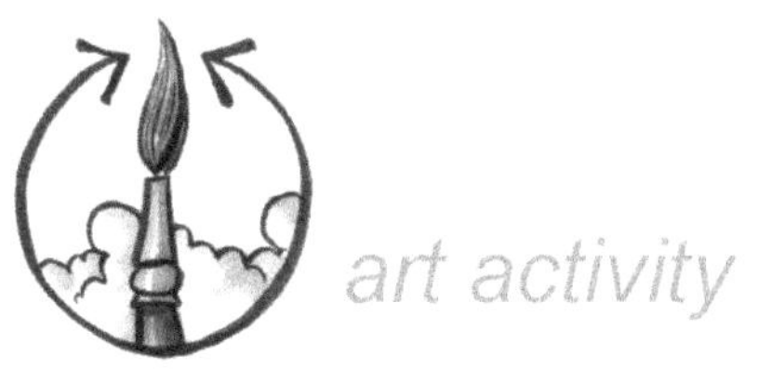

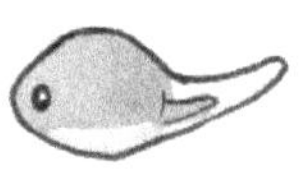

Sailing Off the Edge of the World

Background: Sometimes when we draw, we get to the end of the page and run out of space. We may feel like early explorers who were afraid of sailing off the edge of a flat world. We may wish that we could extend the paper just a bit farther. In this activity, we are going to be making a drawing that could possibly go on forever.

Materials: Pencil or pen, several sheets of paper, Scotch tape.

Directions:

- Find a place to sit and draw. Just about any place will do. There are beautiful and interesting things to see anywhere, if we look closely enough.

- Begin drawing something nearby. Perhaps you will start with a lizard resting on the sidewalk. Draw it nice and large so that you can get all of the details you can see. With the lizard, you will want to get the pattern in its scales and its small blue tongue.

- Keep drawing what is next to the lizard until you run into the edge of your paper.

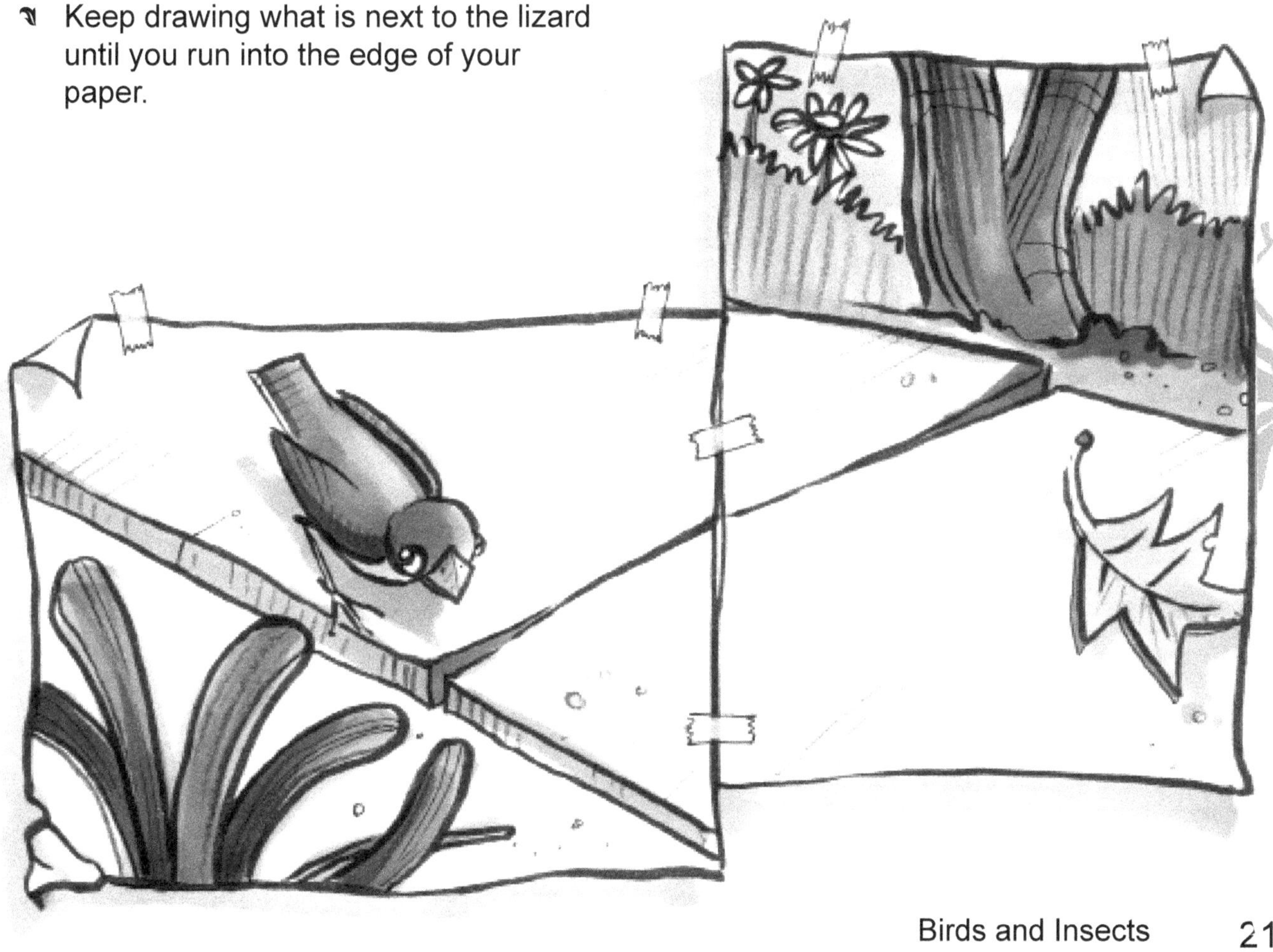

❧ Then, using tape, simply attach a new sheet of paper to the edge, and keep drawing. Maybe on this page you will add the mailbox and some of the flowers above the lizard.

❧ Draw until you reach the edge of this paper and add another. You can branch out in any direction.

❧ Continue adding pages until you have extended the drawing in all of your favorite directions. Don't stop until you have added at least six pages.

Consider This: Would it be possible to include every detail you see? How long would it take? How many sheets of paper would you need? What might the drawing look like?

____

____

____

Going Further: Try adding enough paper so that you can extend your drawing from things that are in front of you to things that are behind you. What do you notice about your drawing?

____

____

____

Try going for a short walk. Make a long drawing in several sheets that shows the whole path of your journey and all your favorite landmarks.

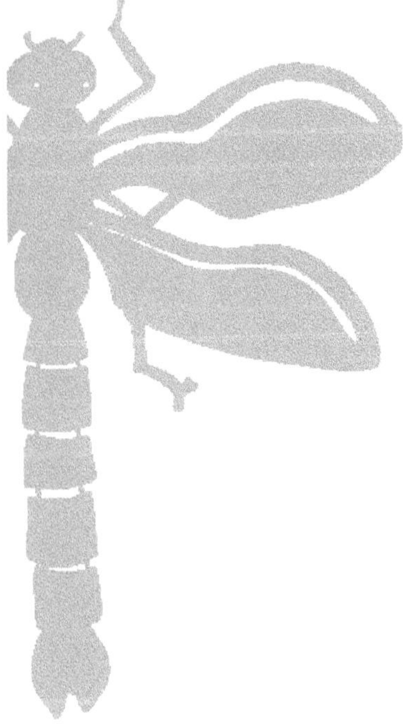

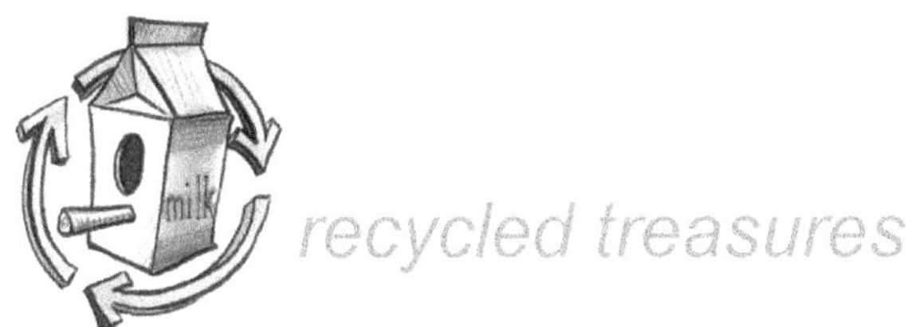

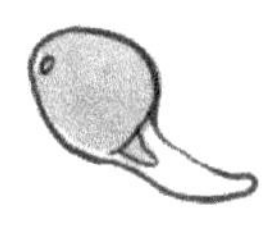

Make Your Own Quill Pen

Background: Quill pens used to be the most common drawing tools. Now that ball-point pens can be found in nearly every junk drawer, they are a rare sight. Quill pens were made from the feathers of birds. The most common pens in the United States used goose feathers because they were large and plentiful. For fine lines and details, people preferred crow quills.

Under the Migratory Bird Treaty Act, almost all native North American birds are protected. So are their eggs and feathers. State and federal permits are required to collect feathers from wild birds. For this project, you can use feathers from domesticated birds like chickens or you can make quill pens from drinking straws or hollow reeds.

Materials: A feather, hollow reed or drinking straw, a sharp knife, scissors, India ink — thinned watercolors or very strong tea will work.

Directions:

- With a sharp knife, cut the feather or drinking straw in a sweeping cut as shown in the drawing.

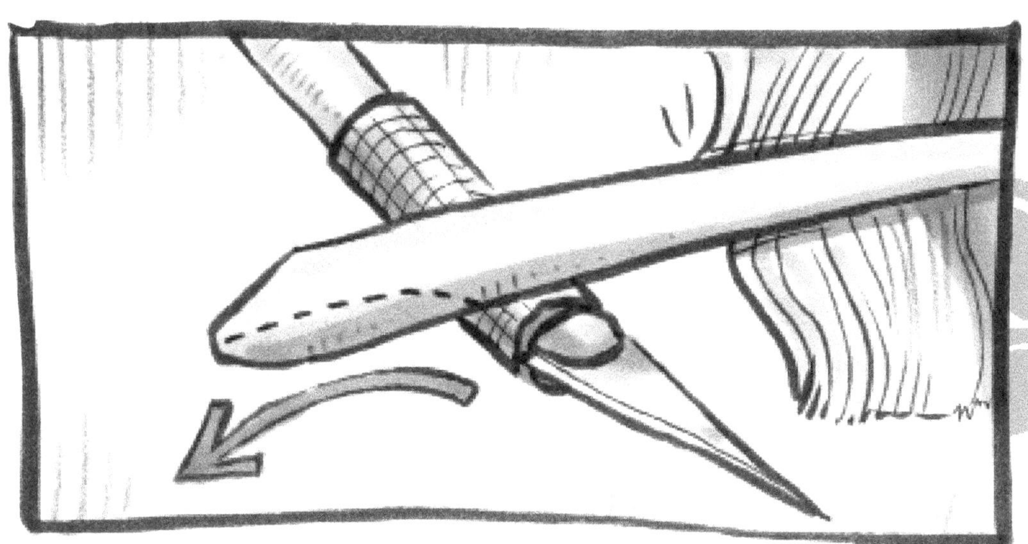

- Make a second cut at an angle to leave a flat edge for a point as shown in the next drawing.

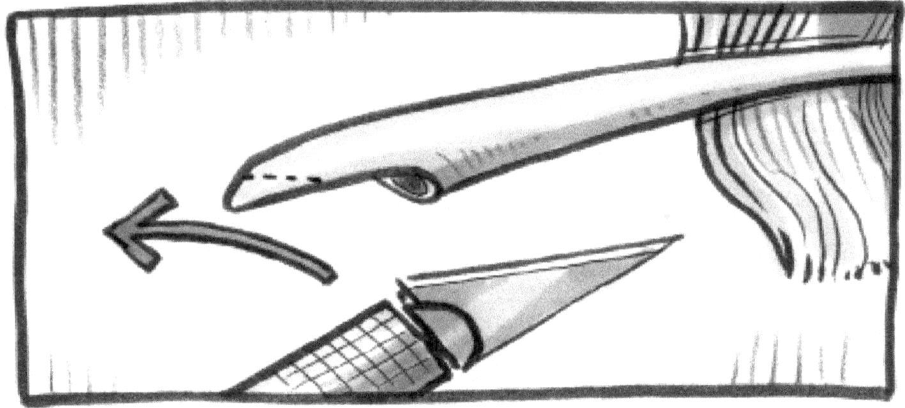

❧ Now, with the tip of a very sharp knife, very carefully split the straw down the center. You can fold it in half gently to create a crease line first. If you gently heat a feather over a hot toaster, it will turn from milky to opaque and will get a bit stronger.

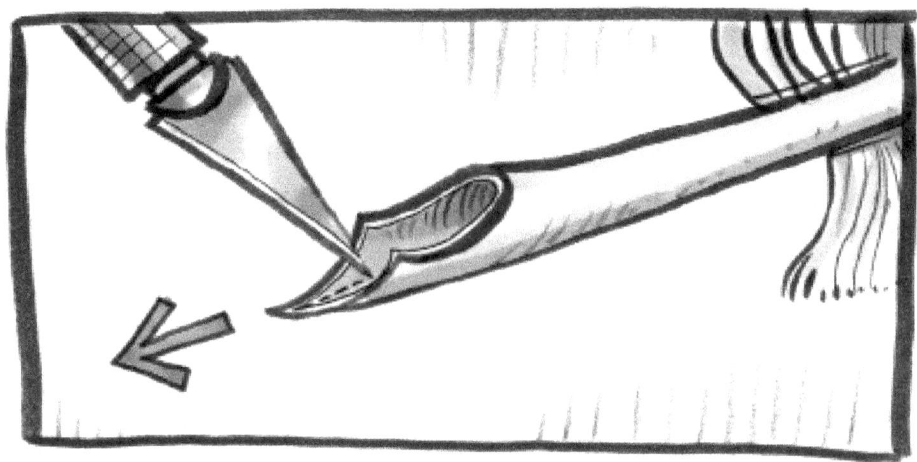

❧ To test your new pen, dip it in ink. If you don't have ink, you can make some brown dye by steeping a few bags of tea in half a cup of boiling water for a half hour. The ink fills the crack in your new pen. As you gently pull the pen, the quills spread and the ink flows onto the paper.

Try This: Using your feather or straw quill, draw a portrait of your favorite type of bird in the box to the right.

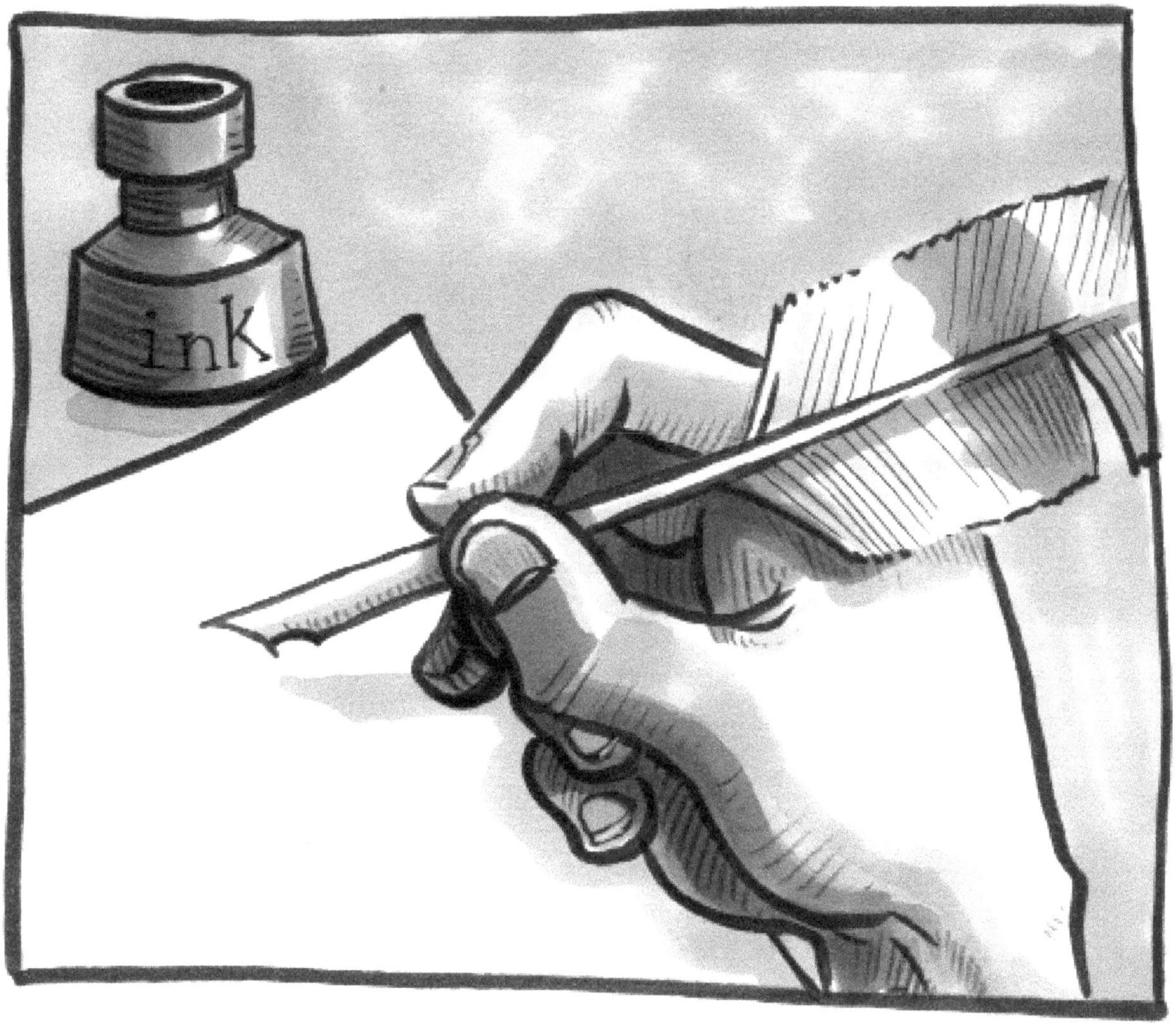

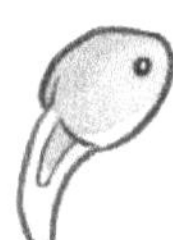

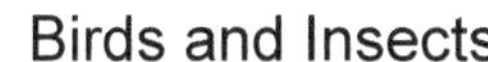

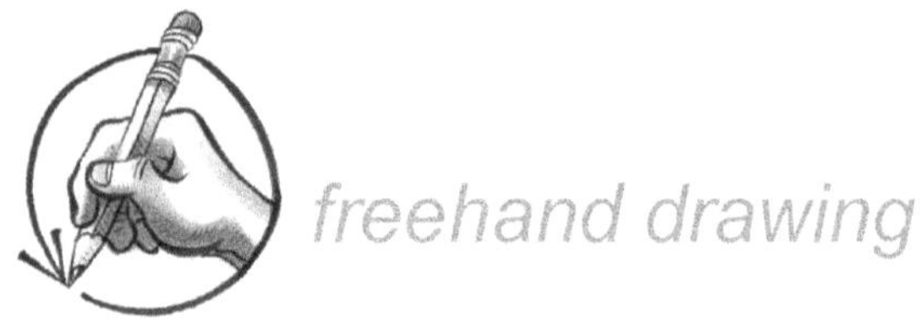

Bird Drawing Step-By-Step: A Mockingbird

Background: Mockingbirds are the musical artists of the forest. They are known for mimicking the songs of other birds and repeating them in creative new arrangements. Mockingbirds have even been known to copy the sounds of car alarms as they sing in the morning.

Directions: Follow along with these steps in the box on page 29. Draw as largely as you can so you have room for all of the details.

- When drawing birds, start with two oval shapes: one for the body and one for the head. Look closely at the bird so that you can draw the ovals in the right size and shape.

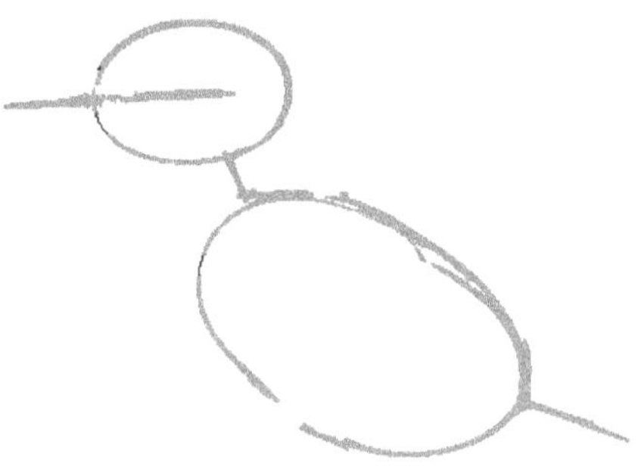

- Draw stick figure legs. Notice that they seem to bend backwards. This is because what we think are the knees are actually ankles and the feet are long toes.

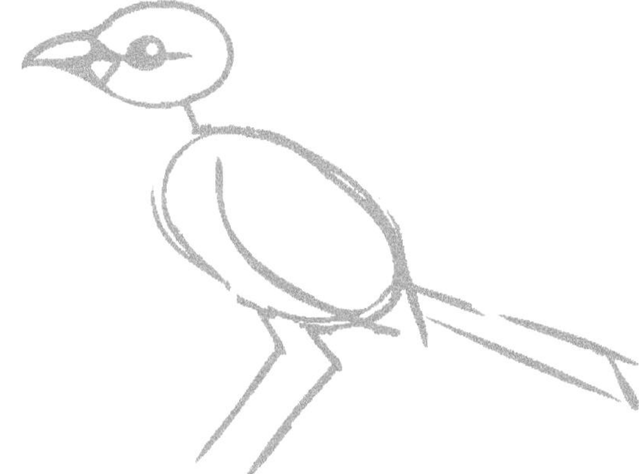

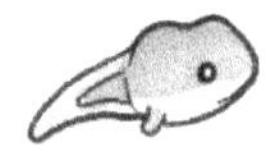

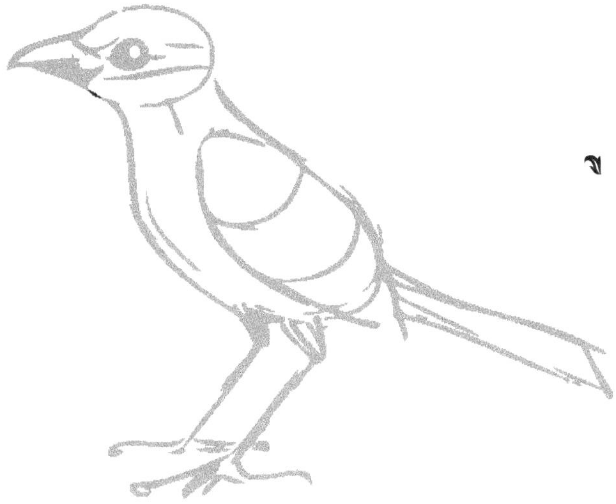

❧ Still working lightly in pencil so you will be able to erase and clean up your drawing, add the eye band and wing stripes. The easiest way to recognize a mockingbird besides by its song is to see the white stripes under its wings when it flies.

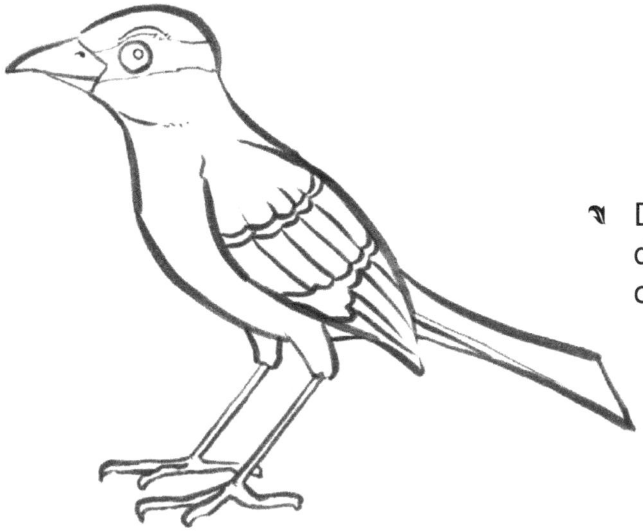

❧ Darken your lines and clean up your drawing with an eraser. Use dark pencil or a black pen.

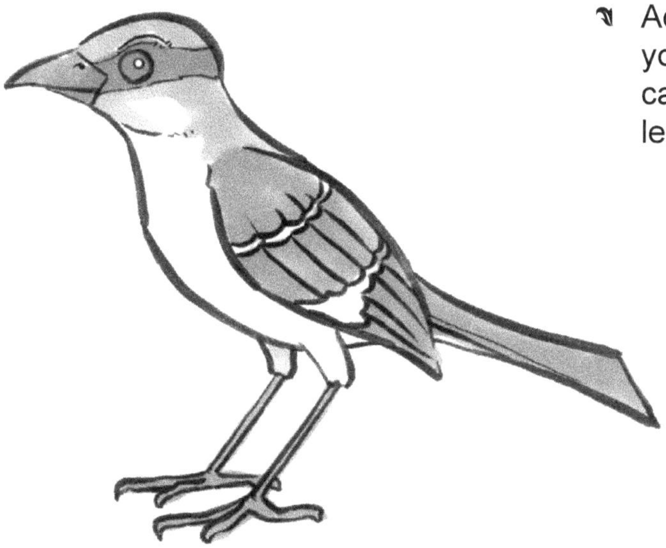

❧ Add shading to your drawing by holding your pencil lightly from the end. You can see a drawing of this in the shading lesson in the next chapter.

Notice how birds' eyes are on the sides of their heads. Why do you think birds would have their eyes on the sides of their heads instead of in front like us?

____
____
____

Look closely at the shape of the beak and feet for clues as to what types of food the bird eats.

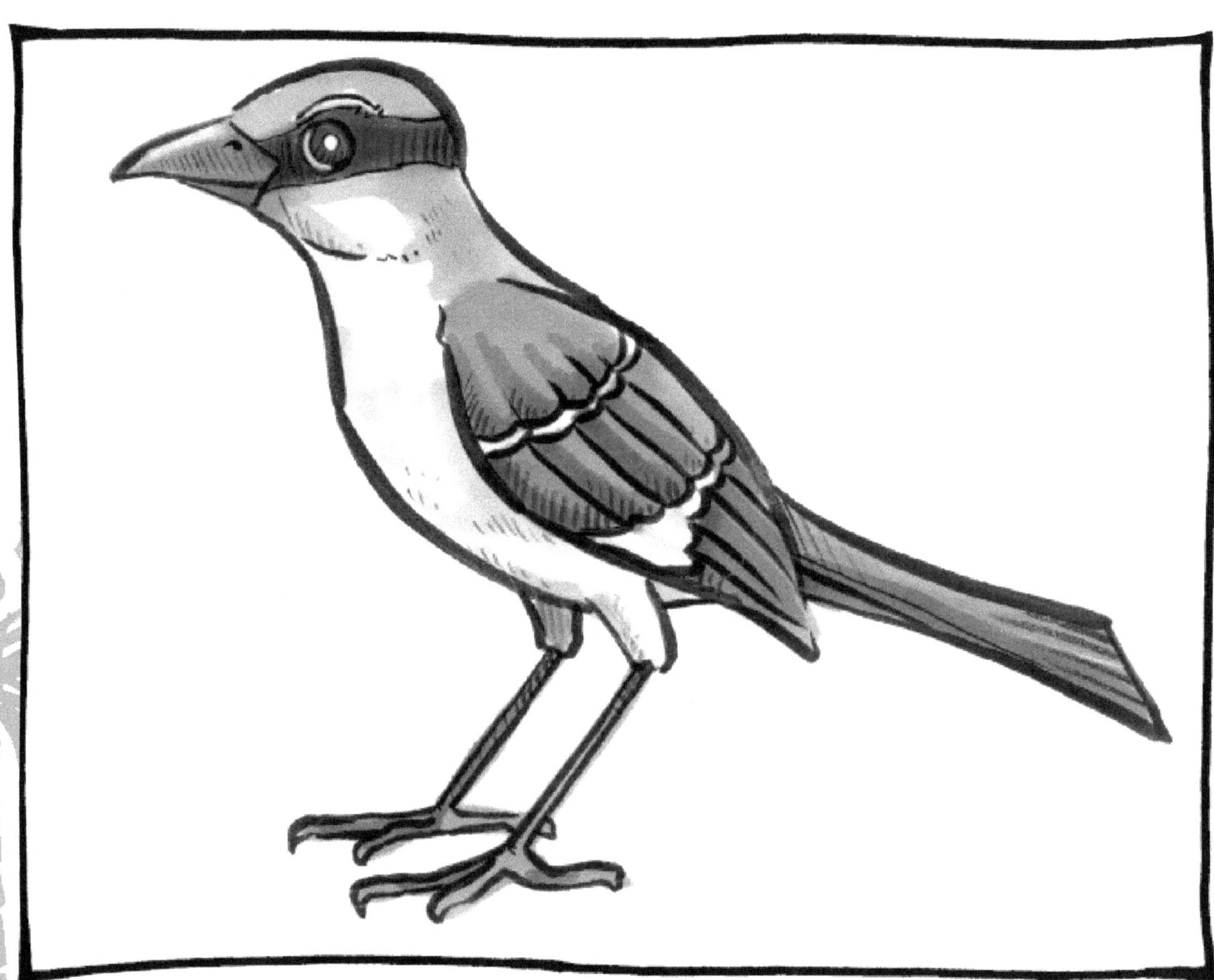

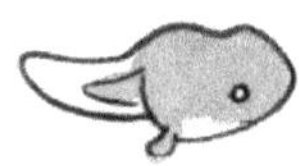

How would you guess carnivorous — meat-eating — beaks differ from seed-eating beaks? What are hummingbirds' beaks designed to do? What would you guess a woodpecker beak would look like?

____
____
____

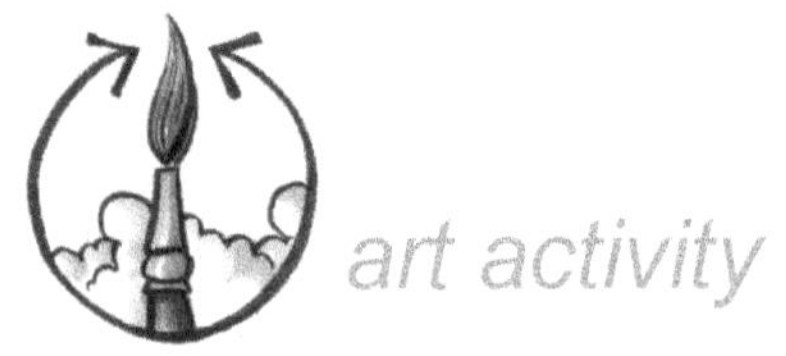

Drawing Wild Birds

Background: Living birds are tricky to draw. As you draw them, they flitter about, eating a bug here, flying up to a branch there, and before you know it, they fly away. All you have drawn is a blurry wing. You can't sneak up on a bird; they are too observant. So, part of learning to draw wild birds is learning to sit still long enough for them to come to you and to be patient.

Materials: Pencil, sketch pad, and patience

Sitting: When we walk into the woods, it is fun to listen to the songs of the birds. Sometimes the bird sounds you hear are not the birds singing their songs. Instead, you are hearing their warning calls to alert all the forest creatures that a dangerous creature is approaching. They are talking about us. Why do you think birds consider people a threat?

If we can settle ourselves in an area where birds like to be and sit quietly for twenty minutes, the birds will calm down again. They will not seem to sense a threat any longer. Sitting still for twenty minutes can be much harder than it sounds, but it is worth the effort. If you do it often, you will see things that you have never seen before.

Directions:

- Walk to an area that has lots of birds early in the morning or near sunset.

- Find a place to sit that isn't too out in the open. Make yourself comfortable.

- Sit as still and silently as you can for at least twenty minutes. Pay close attention to the bird songs and notice how they change over time. Pay attention to all of your senses.

- When a bird comes near, remain still and look at it with your peripheral vision, out the sides of your eyes. Stay calm and breathe naturally, and it will be more likely to stay nearby.

- Follow the steps from the previous lesson, and sketch the bird.

- As you are drawing the bird, try to think of your eyes as a camera. Remember as many details as you can, knowing that this bird could disappear at any time. What colors does it have? What patterns are they in? What is its tail shaped like? How about its beak?

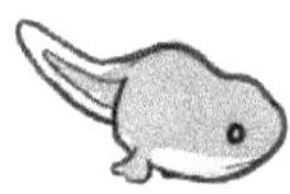

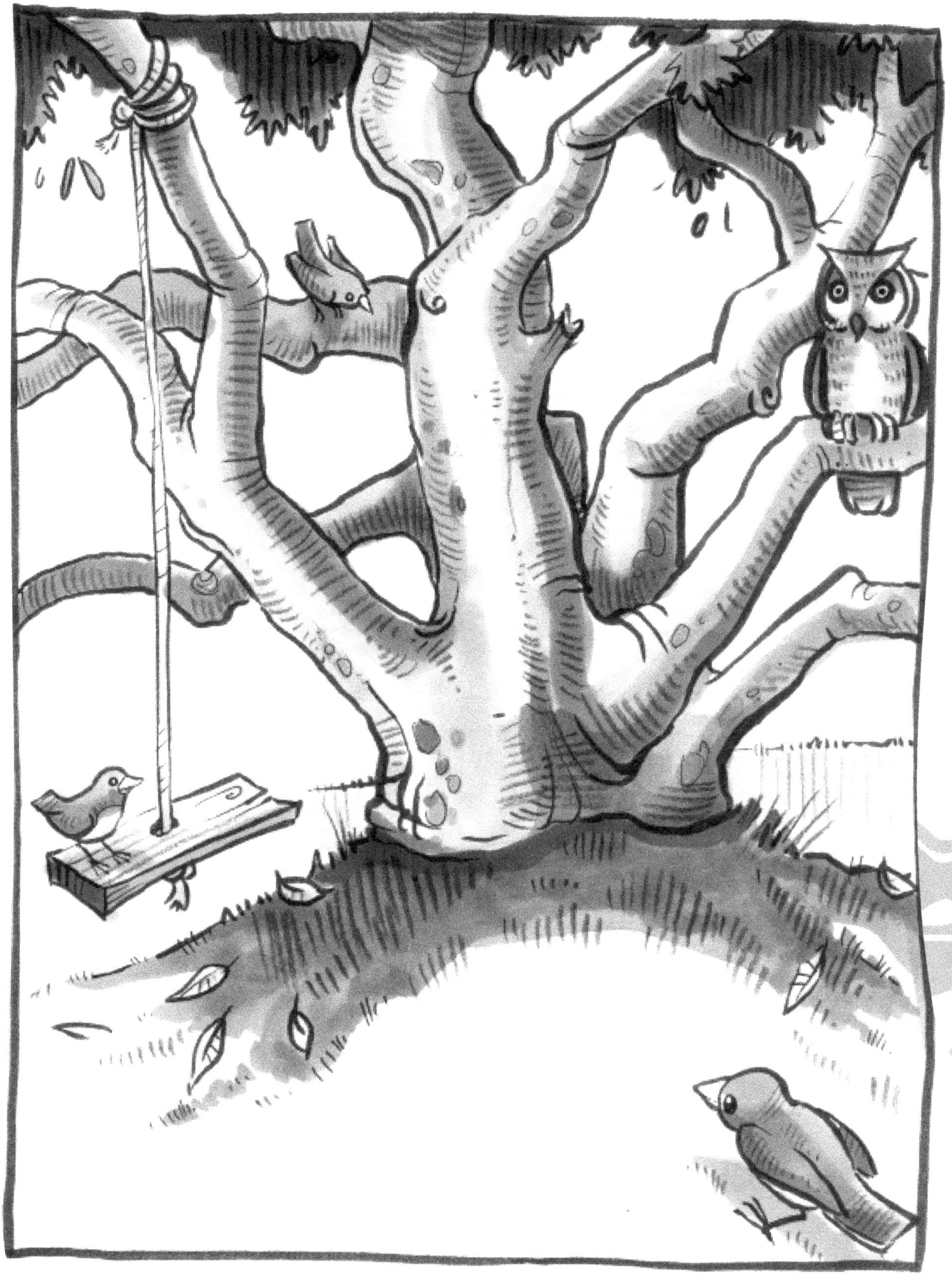

❧ Draw until it disappears.

❧ After you are done sitting, make a list of all the things you noticed. Fill in the senses chart below. List all of the insects, reptiles, birds and animals that you saw.

❧ Working from your sketch, draw a final drawing of your bird in the space to the right.

	Sights	Sounds	Smells	Tastes	Textures
Plants and Trees					
Birds and Insects					
Animals and People					

Date:____

Bird name:____

Place you observed it:_________________________________

A Recycled Birdhouse

Background: Assemblage is a type of sculpture. Assemblage artists use objects and materials that they find and lots of white glue to assemble fun, recycled artworks. The challenge for this project is to create a beautiful, unique birdhouse out of discarded things that you find.

Materials: White glue, water-based latex paint (optional), scrap wood, hammer and nails, and found objects. The goal of this project is not to buy anything. Hunt for all kinds of treasures. They may include things like: corks, plastic toys, springs, wires, popsicle sticks, clothespins, lost checkers, missing buttons, beads, discarded hardware, broken radios, old eyeglass lenses, seed pods, feathers, toilet paper tubes, drinking straws, and whatever else jumps out at you.

Consider This: Birds can be very choosy about the size of their homes. They need a size that gives them enough space, but is small enough that they feel secure and cozy. The door should be as small as possible to keep predators out, yet still allow the bird to come and go easily.

Example: A Western Bluebird nesting box should be 5"x5" wide and 8"-12" tall. The entrance hole should be 1"-1.5" in diameter and placed 6"-10" above the bottom of the box. The box should hang 4-6 feet above the ground.

Directions:

- Choose a bird that you have seen before in your neighborhood. Using the Internet or the library, research birdhouse sizes to find out what size the birdhouse and its entrance should be, and where and how high to hang it.

- Start with a box the appropriate size. You could build one out of scrap lumber, or you could use a found object. A large oatmeal box could work for a bluebird. The outside should be sealed with water-based latex paint so the cardboard won't fall apart in the rain.

- Go on a scavenger hunt for materials. Look in the garage. Look in the recycle bin. Look at the drawings to get ideas of the things you could add to your house.

- Lay out the stuff you have collected. In the frame provided, make a sketch of what you imagine your final birdhouse will look like. You are an architect, and this will be your blueprint. You could make it look like a miniature replica of your own house. It could be an outdoor cuckoo clock, with a cuckoo that is free to wander. It could be the head of a hungry cat with the hole going into the cat's mouth.

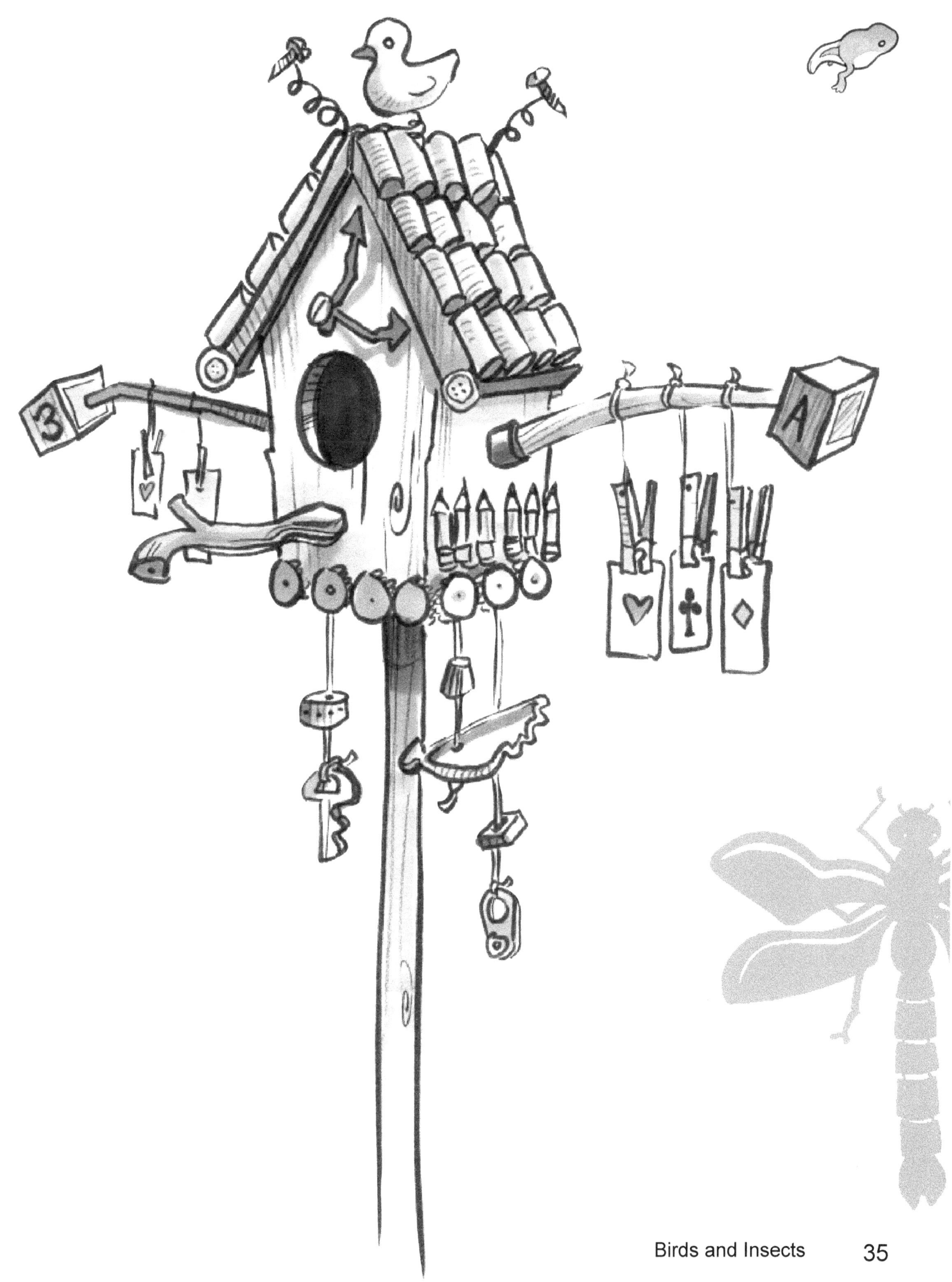

◥ Using lots of glue, create your birdhouse. Sealing it with dull light-colored water-based latex paint such as tan or grey can make it even more beautiful and will help it hold up to the weather. Be careful not to paint the entrance hole or the inside of the box.

More To Consider: In what location do you think your birdhouse would be the most likely to attract some feathered friends? How high off the ground should it be to keep clever cats from reaching in the door? Will it be sturdy if the winds pick up? How can you make sure the inside will not get too hot for the baby birds?

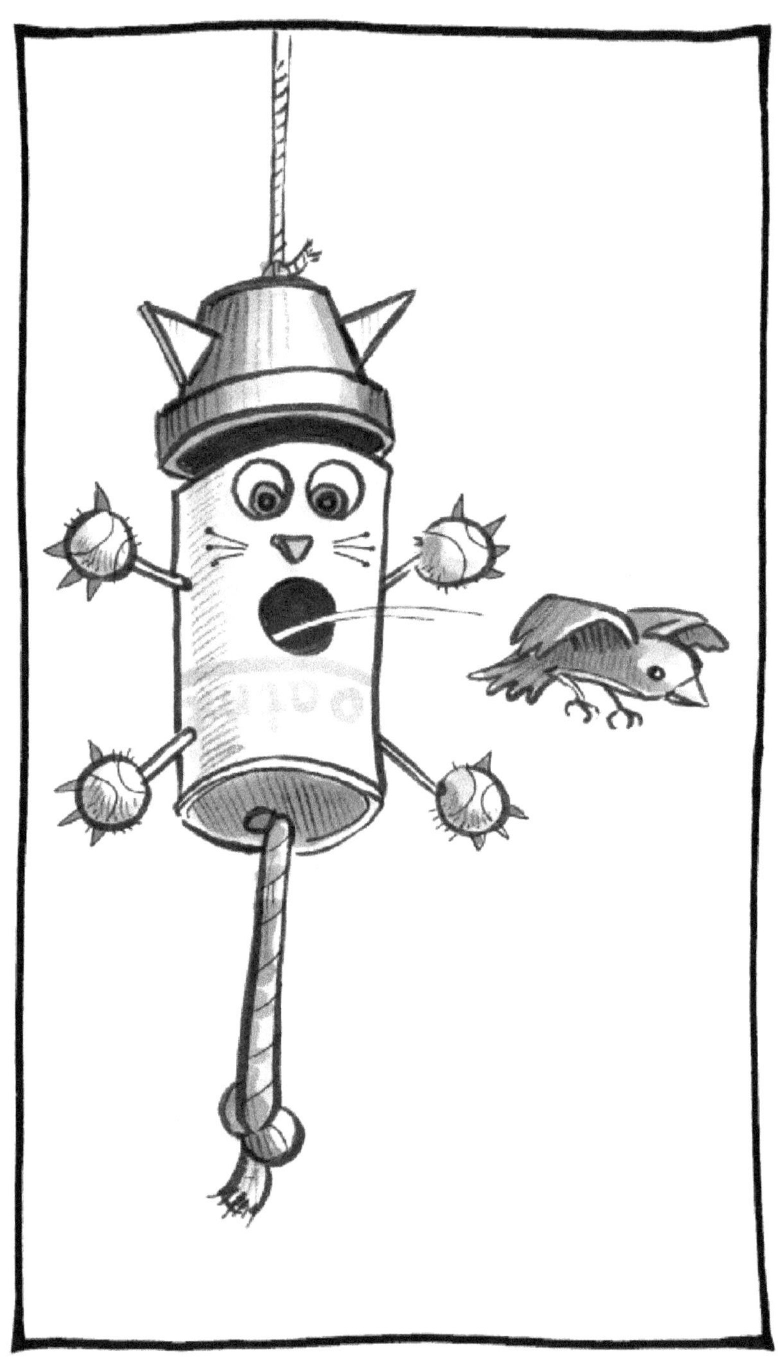

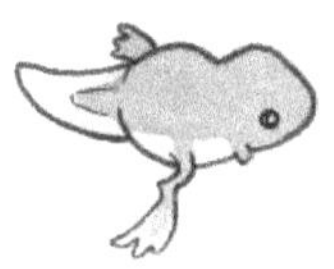

Focus on James Audubon

John James Audubon was born in Haiti in 1785 and lived in France from the time he was three. As a child he showed a strong interest in nature and spent much of his time walking into the local woods. He often returned with nests or eggs, which he made drawings of. At age eighteen, he came to America so that he would not have to fight in the Napoleonic Wars.

In the United States, Audubon enjoyed a life of fishing, hunting, drawing and making music. His interest in birds deepened, and he felt the urge to record all the American birds, drawing them in a style that made them appear lifelike. Audubon experimented with bird banding. He tied strings around the legs of Eastern Phoebes that he caught, and the following season he noticed that the same birds returned each year.

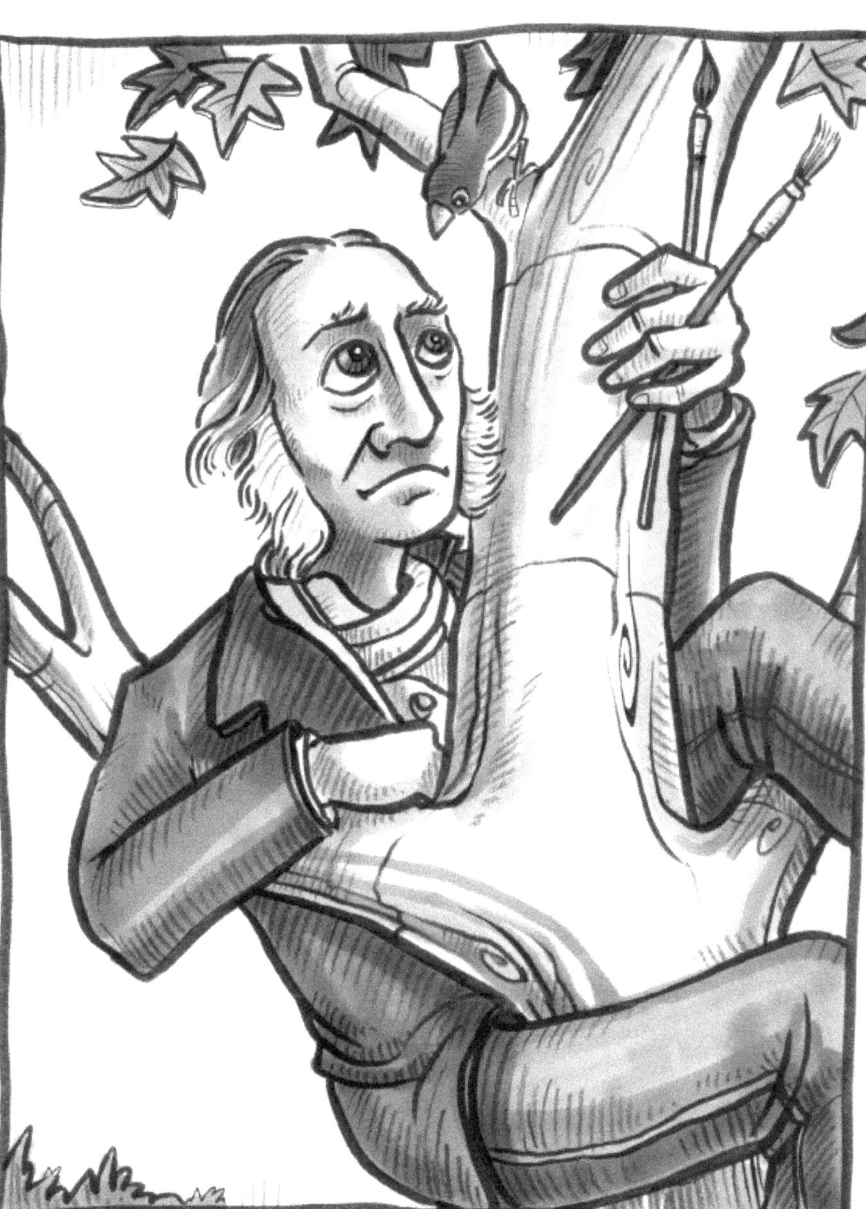

Audubon is best known for his Birds of America portfolio. The portfolio contains over four hundred etchings of different birds that Audubon caught and drew. They are in full color. He was an outstanding hunter and killed most of the birds he drew in the book with a bow and arrow. This way, he was able to see details and forms that he would not have been able to observe from a distance. It is ironic that he had to kill something that he loved so much. He is now known as the symbol of bird conservation, and the Audubon Society is named in his memory.

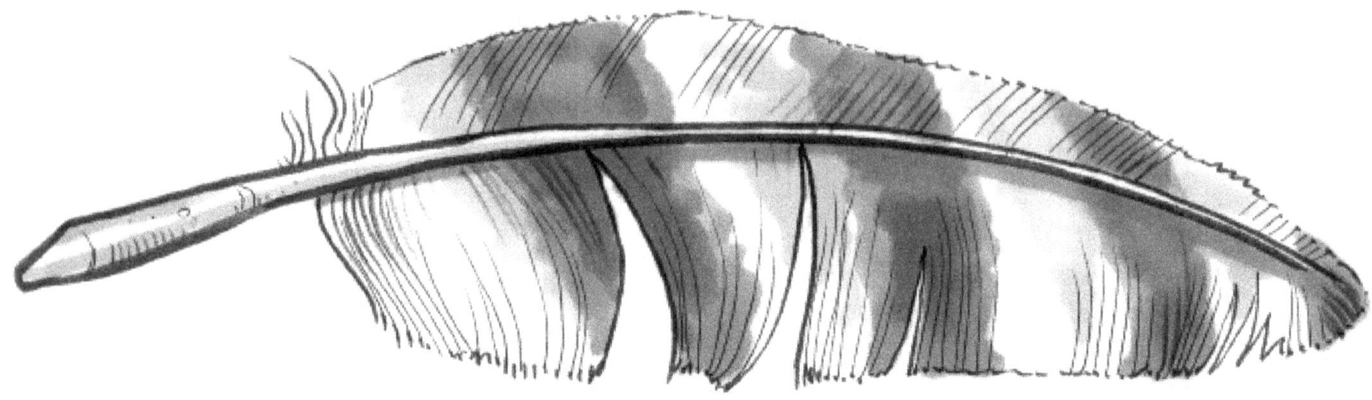

Consider This: John James Audubon made people aware of hundreds of bird species that live in our country. Many have since gone extinct. Even though he killed them to draw them, do you think he might have also helped save other birds? How?

____

____

____

____

____

Some people cannot fully enjoy going to a natural history museum or even a zoo without feeling some remorse that the animals or birds found there would be better off if they were left alone in the wild. Do you think the lives of these captive animals might in some way help their relatives in the wild? How?

____

____

____

____

Image Hunt: Search the Internet for some of John James Audubon's bird images. Look for one of his drawings of a bird that you know visits your neighborhood. Try to copy his drawing to the best of your ability.

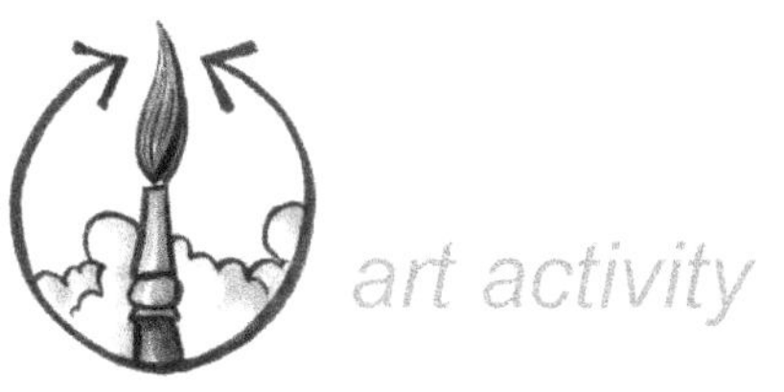 *art activity*

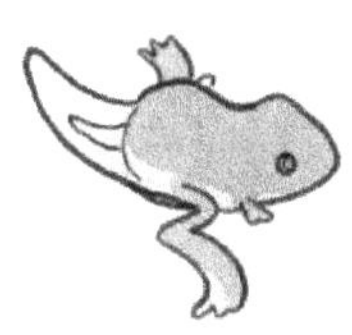

A Bug's-Eye View

Background: The closer you get to something, the more detail there is to see. It can be fascinating to go exploring while lying on your stomach peering through a magnifying glass. A lawn can turn into a forest filled with wild insects. A pond can become an enormous lake swimming with water creatures. A rock can become a mountain. In this project, you will be making a large drawing of something very small.

Materials: Drawing materials such as colored pencils, a small pencil sharpener, a magnifying glass.

Directions:

- Spend a long time exploring your world with a magnifying glass. Get on your hands and knees. Hunt for insects. Peer into flowers. Pull back the top layer of mulch on the soil and see what you find beneath. Turn over rocks and look at your discoveries up close. Be sure to put the mulch and the rocks back in place as you found them.

- When you have found a place that you would like to draw, begin drawing on page 41. Draw things so large that they cannot fit on the page without being cut off by the border. This will help you have a strong composition.

- Keep your pencils sharp, and try to exaggerate the textures of the objects that you are drawing. If they are bumpy, make them bumpier. If they are hairy, make them hairier. Try to get as many details as possible.

- Share your drawing and the place where you drew it with a friend.

Consider This: There are microscopic worlds living here among us. It is said that one tablespoon of soil has more organisms in it than there are people living on the earth. What purpose do you think all of those organisms in the dirt might serve? What do they eat?

____

____

____

____

____

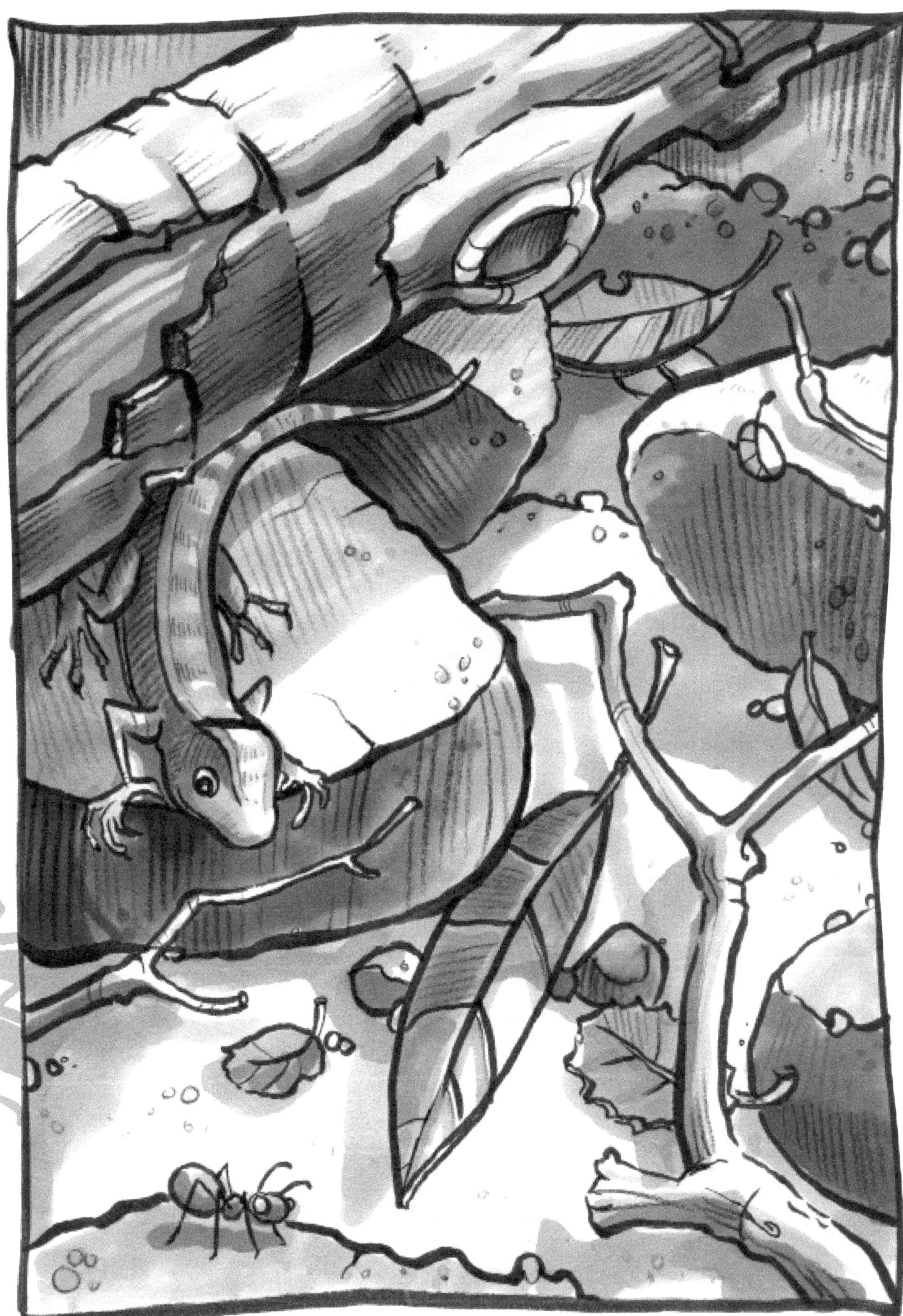

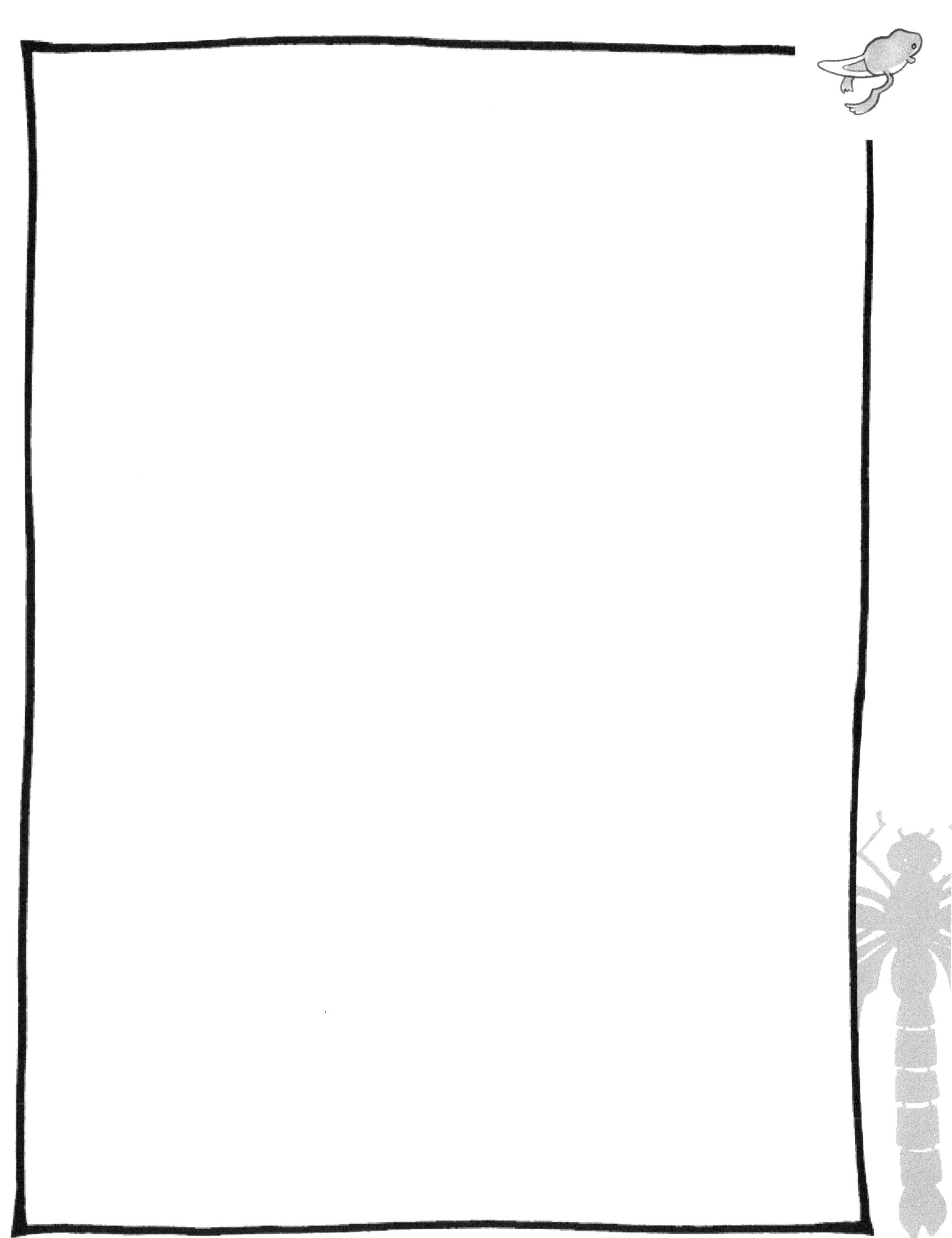

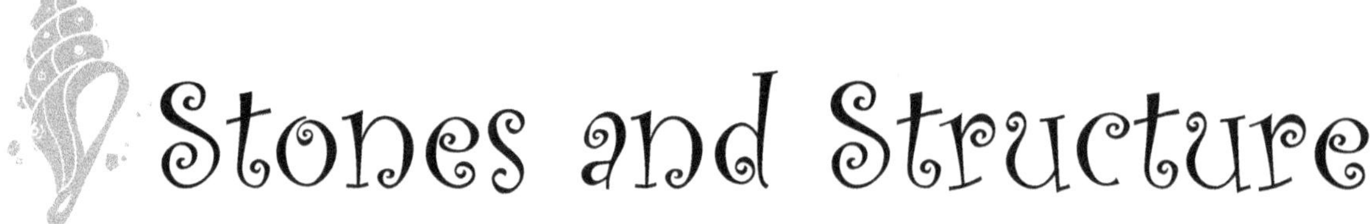

Stones and Structure

Have you ever tried to draw a pinecone? It can seem like a really complicated shape and can be a bit overwhelming until you learn to look at the spirals that wrap around it.

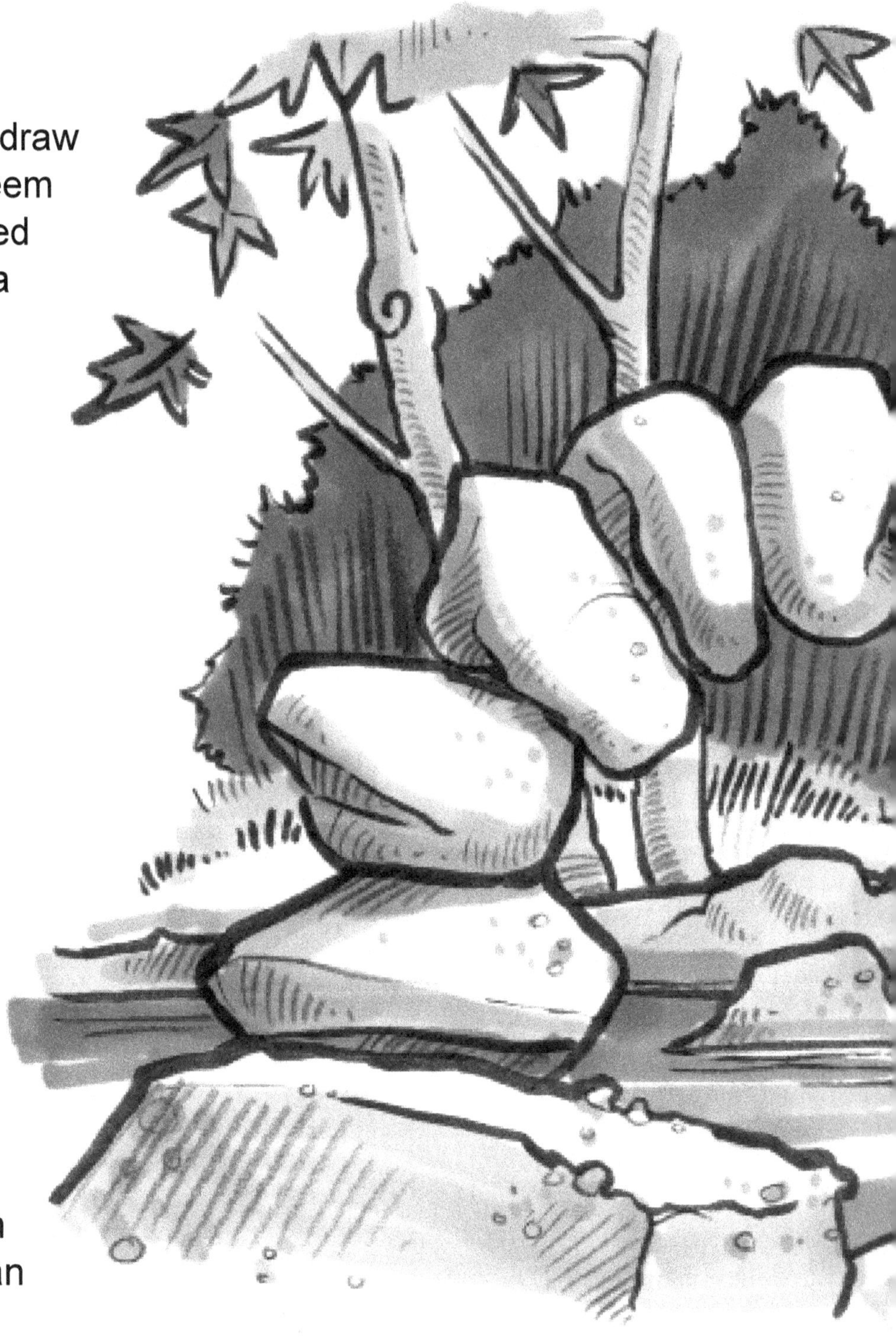

This is a chapter about learning to see patterns, structure, and design. Artists study the way things grow so they can draw them realistically. You will use X-ray vision to imagine the skeletons that support things, give them their shapes and make them move. Once you have drawn something, you will understand it on a much deeper level than

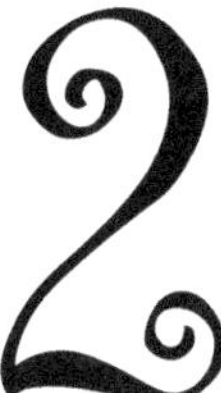
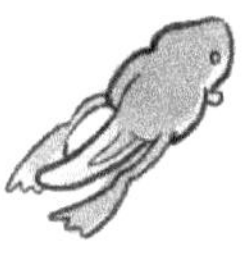

you did before. You will stack and balance rocks and find beauty in how one thing supports another in this world.

Like artists, engineers and inventors also learn a lot by looking at the structure of nature. It was by studying the wings of birds and the ways birds flew that the Wright brothers designed the first airplane. Sometimes it is hard to tell engineers and inventors from artists. They both love to look closely at the world and create things that have never been made.

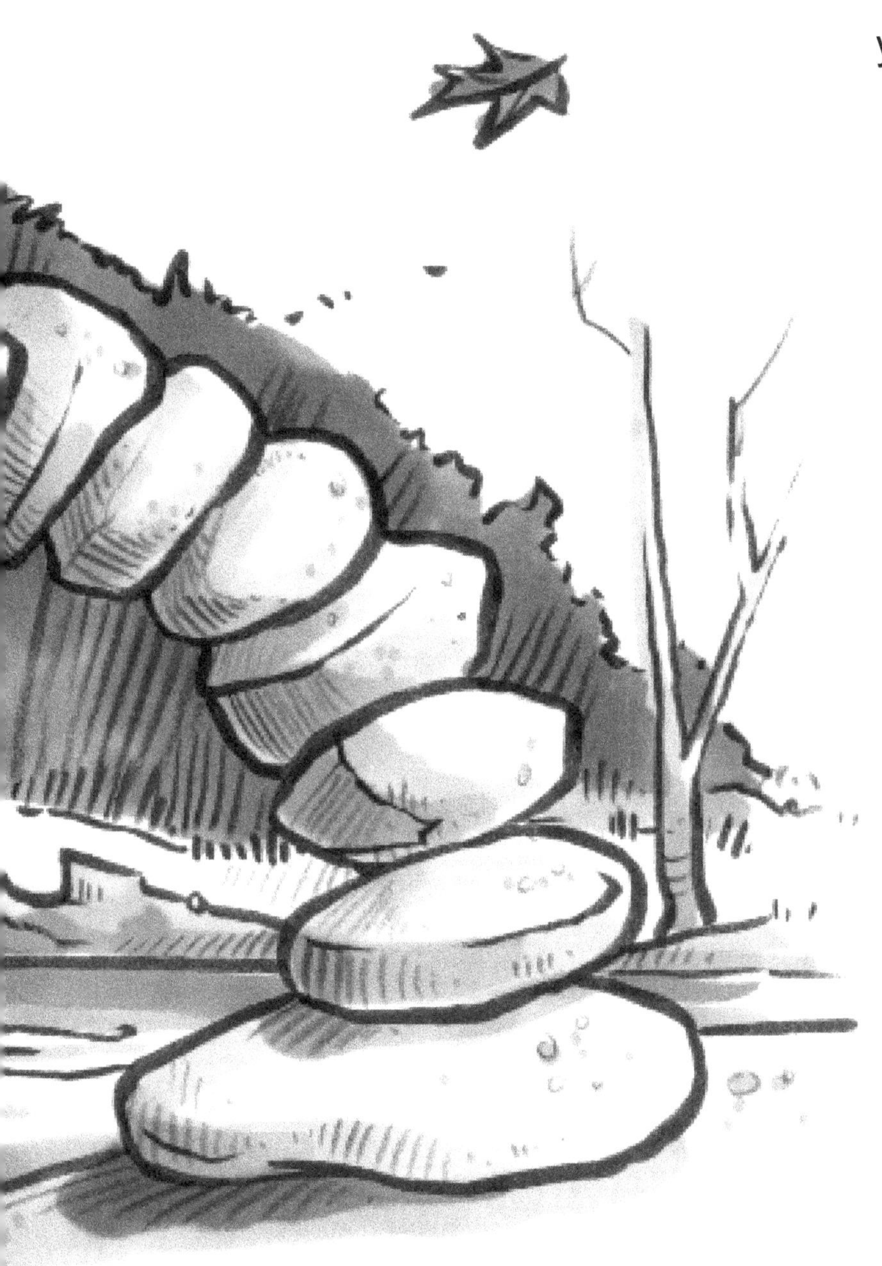

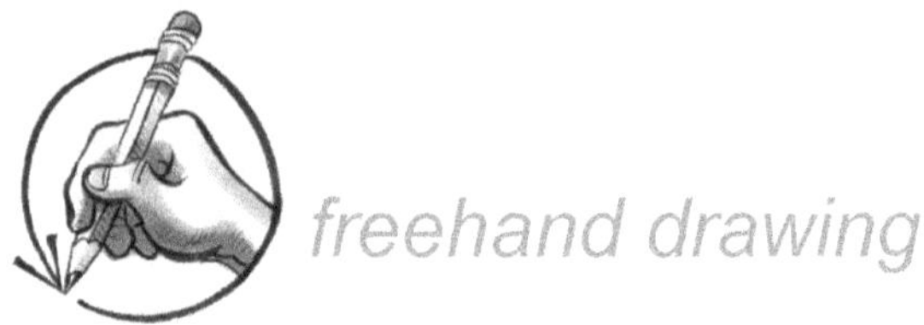

Drawing Texture Step-By-Step

Background: Texture in art means making things look on paper like they would feel if you touched the real object. Texture adds detail and makes people want to reach out and touch your drawings. In this project, you will create several types of texture.

Directions: In the square to the right, follow the steps to transform the sketch into a textured landscape.

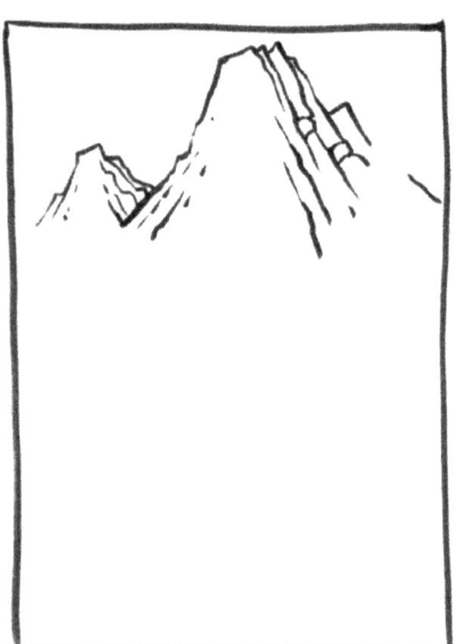

❧ Begin by darkening the mountains and giving them lines that represent cracked and broken stones. Think of the way water washes down the mountainsides and carves canyons and gullies.

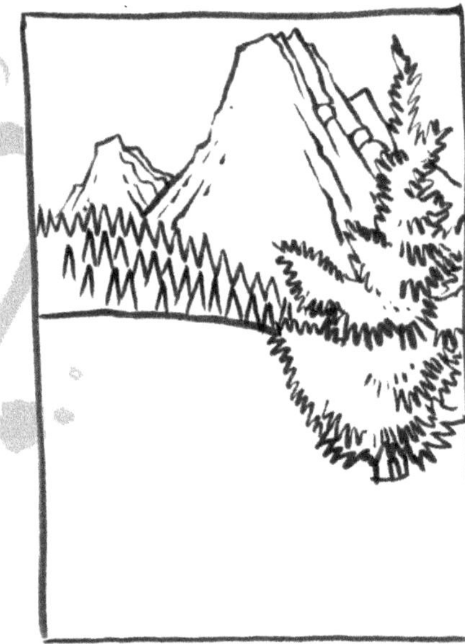

❧ Using repeated points and short, sharp lines, create textures for the distant pine forest and for the pokey needles on the pine tree.

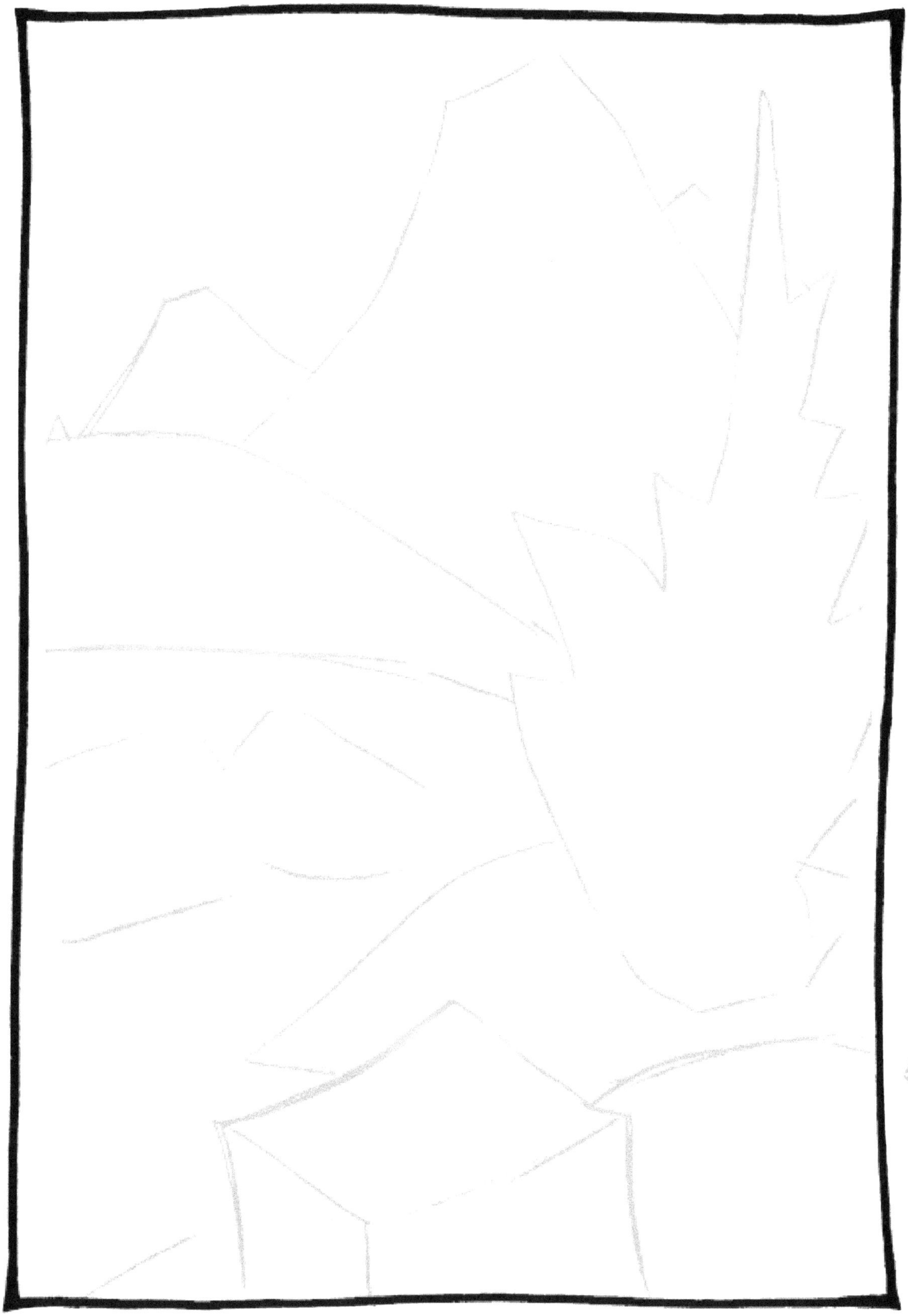

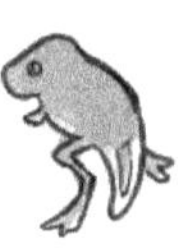

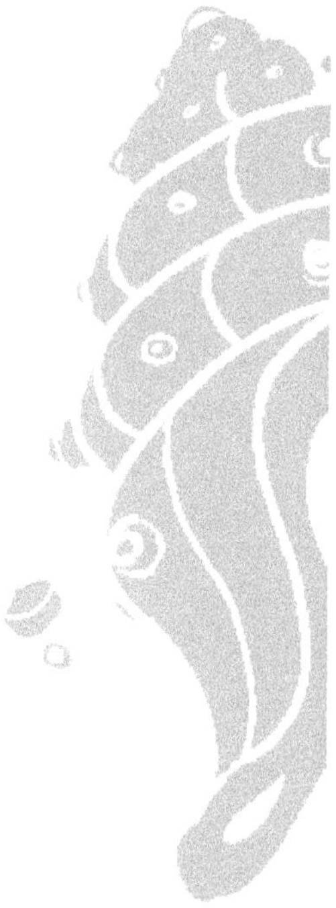

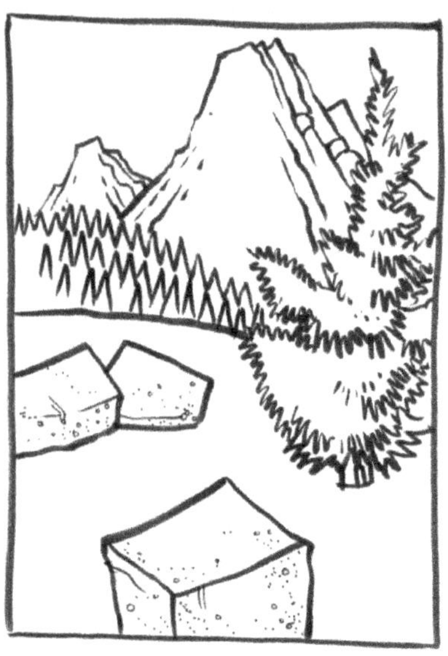

⤵ Darken the texture of the rocks, then add small, pebbly textures of circles and dots to make them look rough.

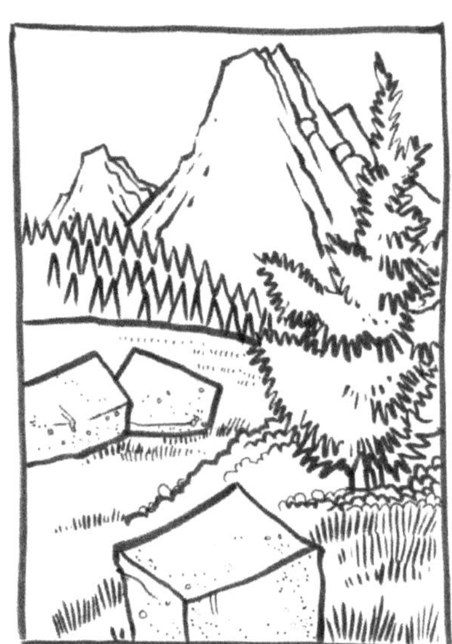

⤵ Finally, add textures to imply earth and grass in the spaces between the objects. Using your pencil or some watercolors, add shading to your drawing to give it some depth.

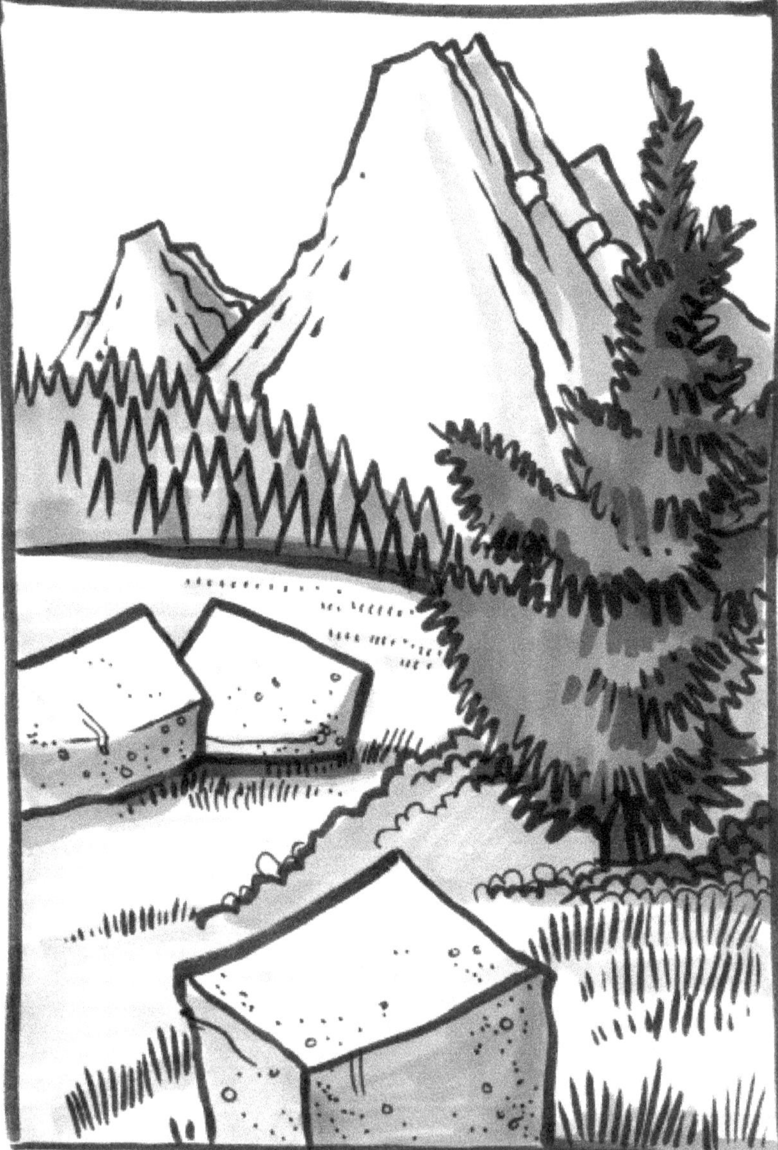

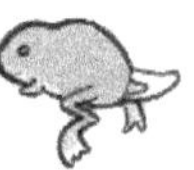

ow, go exploring outdoors for a nice place to sit and observe a local l
scape. Think carefully about what types of marks you can use to imply the
textures in the scene. Make a textured drawing of the scene in the box below.
Show a friend, and see if they can find the place you were drawing just by looking
at your artwork.

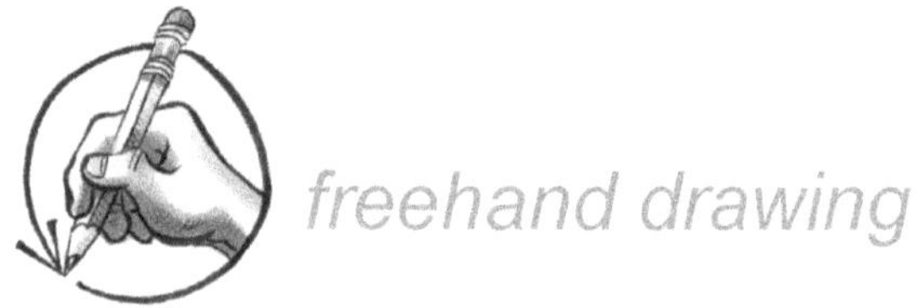

Still Life With Rocks

Background: A still life is a collection of objects that an artist arranges and then draws or paints. Adding shadows to a drawing gives a sense of light and helps it look three-dimensional. Round rocks and sticks create good forms for learning to observe and draw shadows. They make the perfect still life, because what holds still better than a rock or a stick?

Materials: Soft pencil or charcoal, pencil sharpener, desk lamp, round rocks, sticks and paper for a still life.

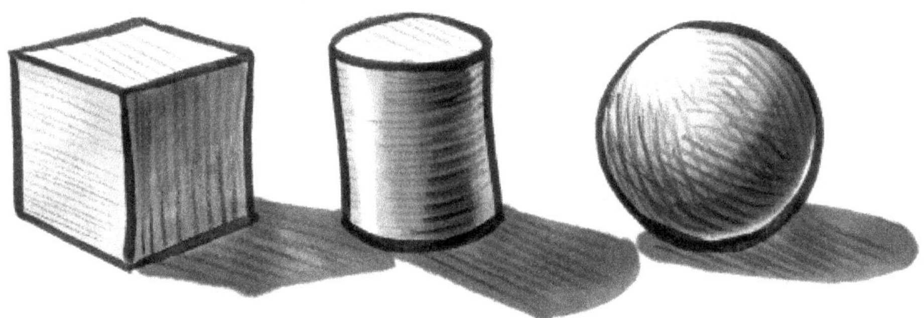

Observation: Look at these three basic forms above. There is a sphere, a cube and a cylinder. Notice how the shading changes very gradually from black to grey to white. When a drawing has many shades of grey, it is said that it has many values. Notice how the lines follow the curves of the objects. These details help give form to the shapes.

Directions:

- Using the flat shapes below, try to copy the shading patterns. It is helpful to hold your pencil near the eraser as shown in the drawing on page 50, and to use light pressure. You want to build up values slowly. The more values you can create from dark to light, the more realistic your shadows will appear.

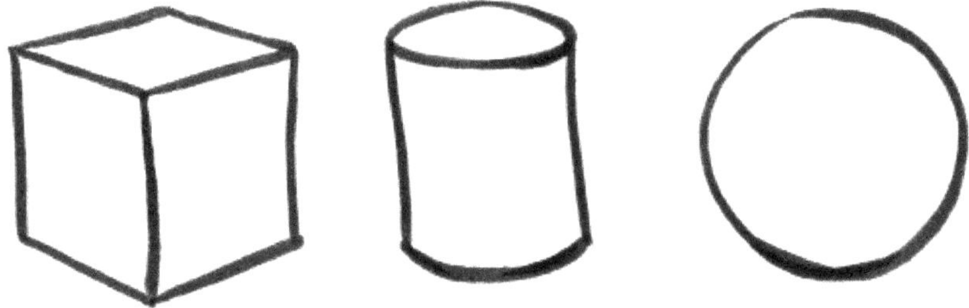

❧ Now you are going to set up a still life of rocks and sticks. Find several rocks and sticks that have different shapes and textures.

❧ Lay a piece of white paper on a table. Arrange your rocks and sticks on the paper. You could arrange them in an interesting pattern or pile them so they look like they fell together naturally. Keep it simple for this first drawing.

❧ Dim the lights in the room, and shine a desk lamp on the objects.

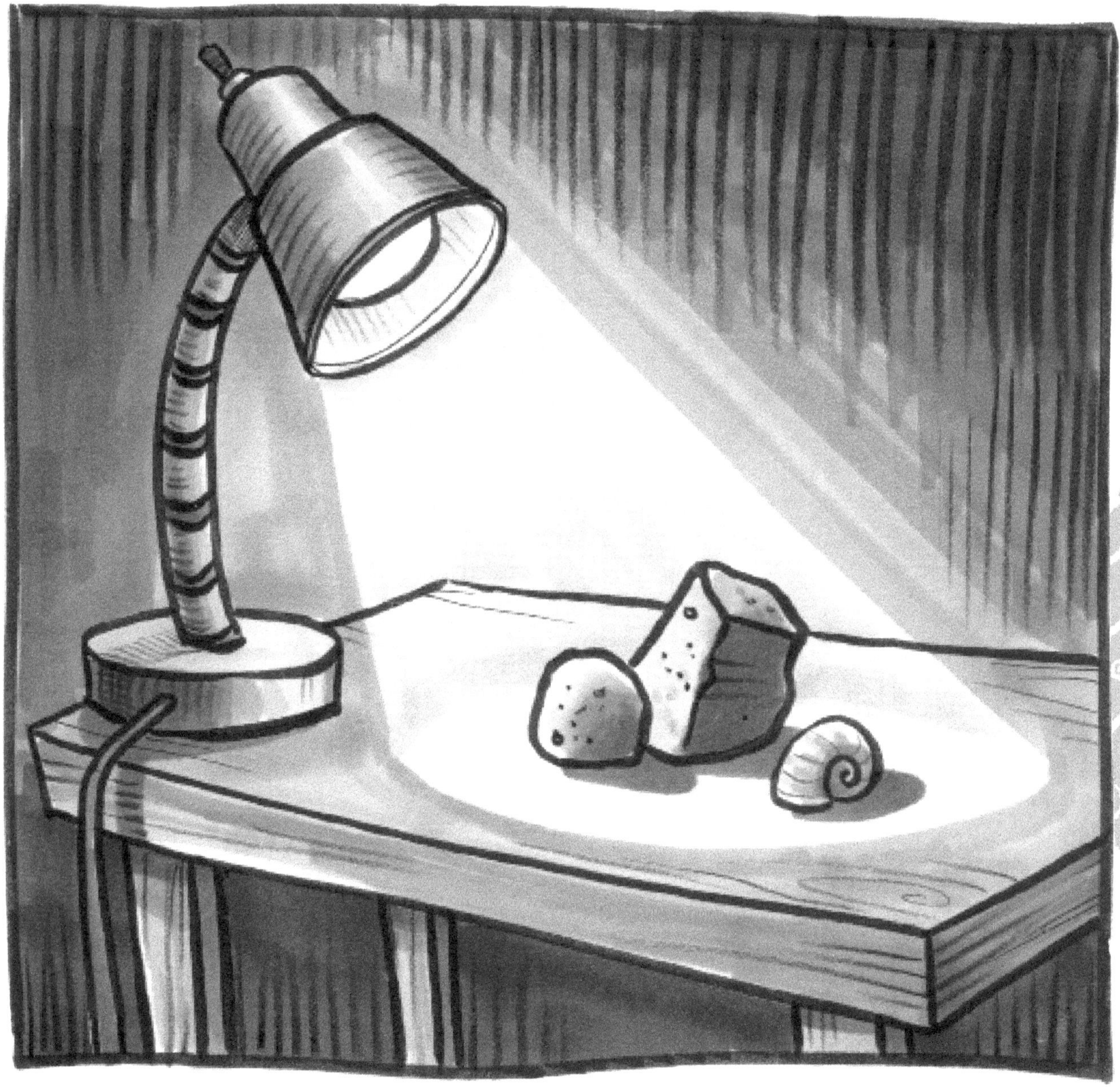

❧ Now, look closely at the shadows on these objects. Compare them to the sphere, cube and cylinder on this page 48. What similarities do you see?

❧ Now, draw these objects nice and large in the space to the right. Not everything has to fit in your frame. The drawing can look more interesting if some of the rock shapes are cut off by the paper's edge.

❧ Now, sharpen your pencil again, and hold it from the back. While closely observing the shadows, see if you can copy them. Try to let your drawing get quite black in the shadows and have many values as it goes from white to black.

Consider This: The next time you go outdoors to make a drawing, think of the sun as a giant desk lamp in the sky. Do the trunks of trees and large boulders reflect the same types of shadows you observed on your tabletop at home? Which of the shapes on page 48 do they look like the most: the sphere, the cube, or the cylinder?

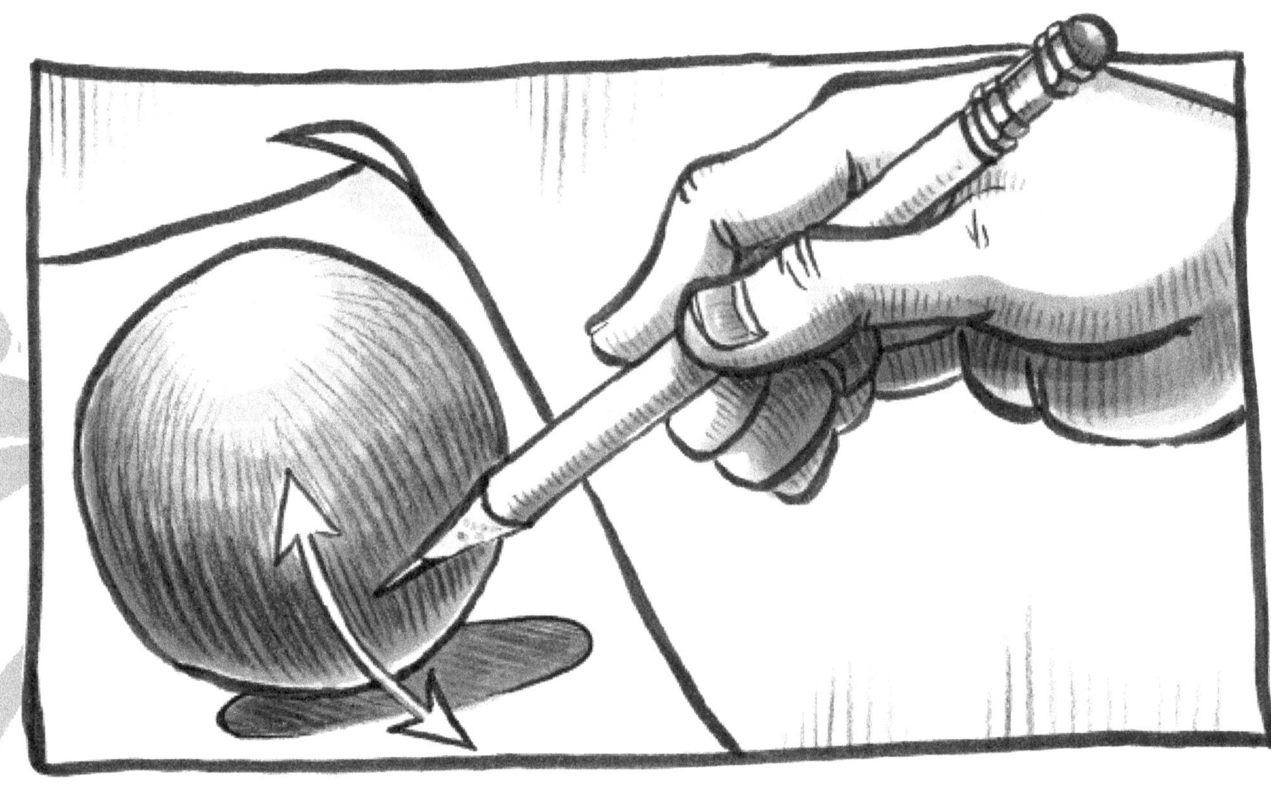

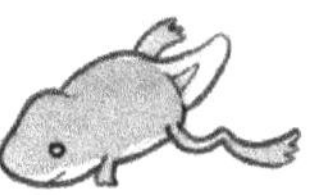

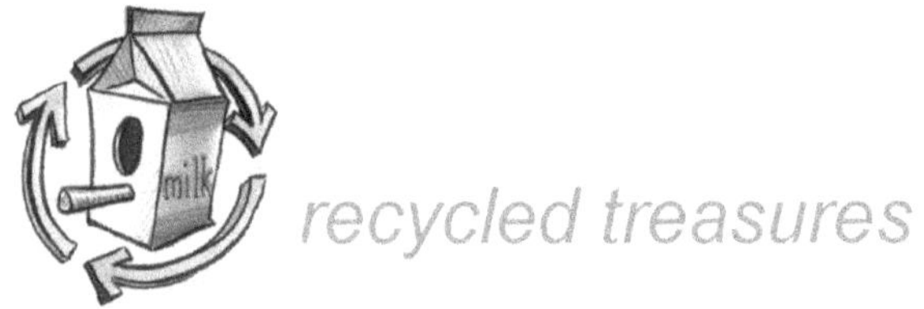

X-ray Vision: Skeleton Sculptures

Background: When drawing animals, artists find it helpful to imagine what their skeletons would look like. Artists often draw stick figures to help them begin their drawings. In the drawing lessons in the first chapter, you learned to build complicated drawings over simple shapes and lines.

Sculptors also begin with skeletons made of wire, called armatures. In this project, you will make an armature in the form of an animal, and then build the body around it with clay or paper mache.

Materials: Pencil, wire, wire cutters, clay, cardboard, newspaper, white glue, paint, and found objects.

Directions:

- Begin by deciding on an animal that you would like to sculpt. Using the Internet, search for two images: one of this animal's skeleton and one of the whole animal.

- Draw the skeleton in the box below.

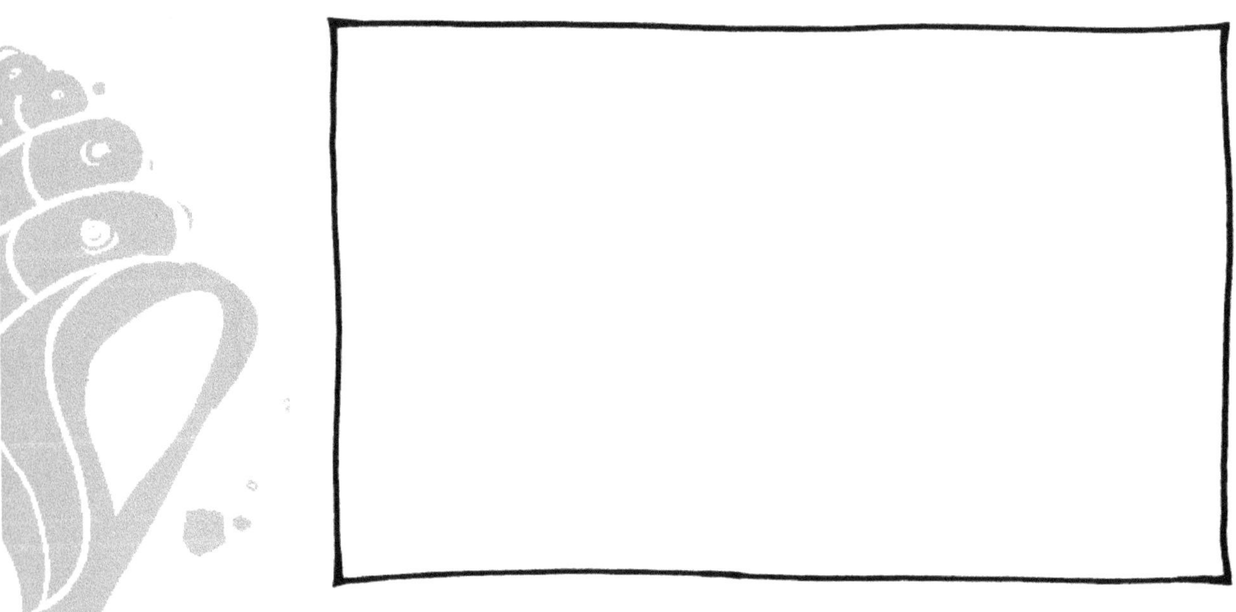

- Using the wire, clay, cardboard, and whatever else seems like it would work, build the skeleton for your animal. Think of all the parts of the skeleton that can bend, and try moving these until you have found a pose that is balanced and interesting.

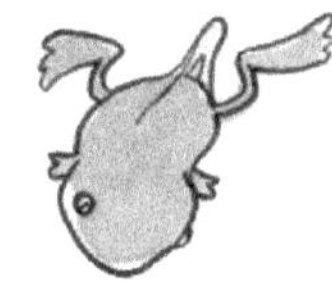

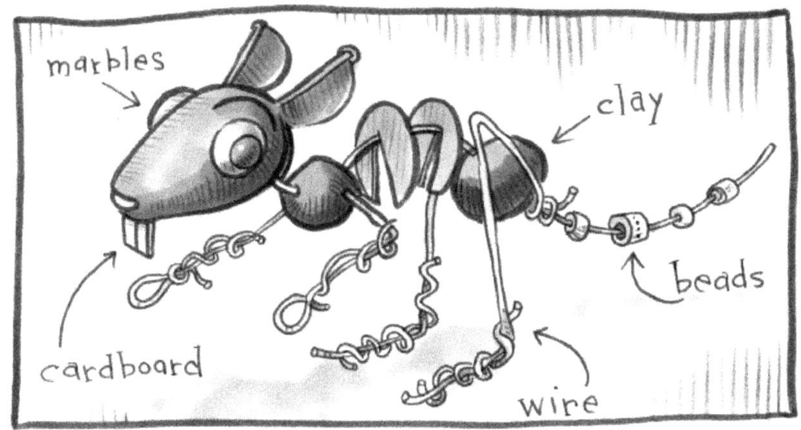

❧ You will now begin fleshing out your animal by adding air-dry clay or paper mache. To make paper mache, mix one part water with two parts white glue. Cut sheets of newspaper into thin strips and soak these in this thinned paste. Remove the excess glue by pulling strips through your fingers and then lay them over your armature in several layers.

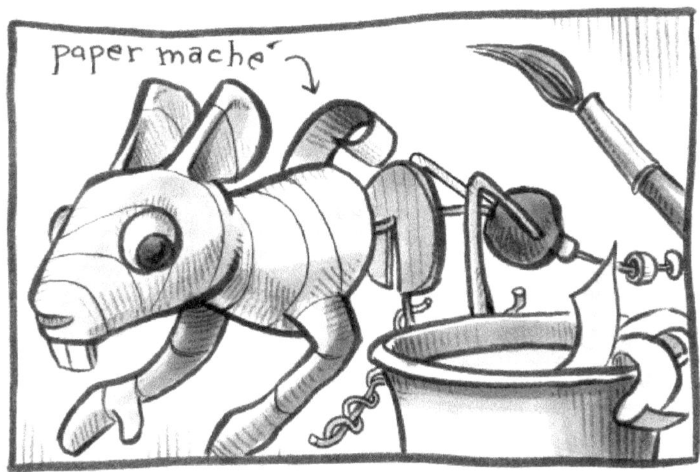

❧ After your sculpture has dried, you can paint it. Try setting your sculpture outside in a natural setting and taking a close-up picture. Try placing it in different environments and see how this changes its appearance.

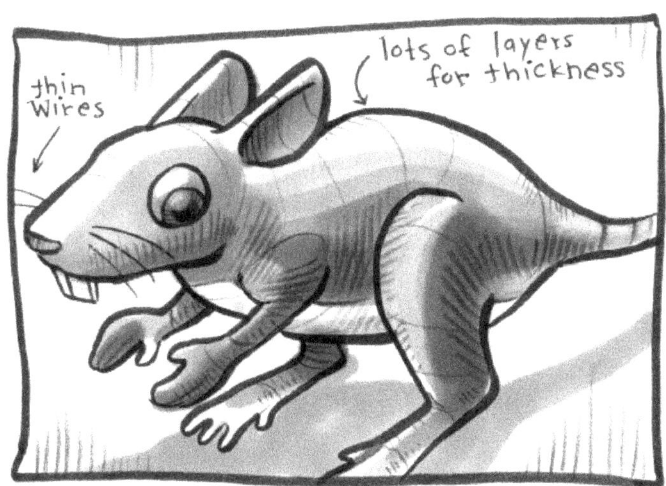

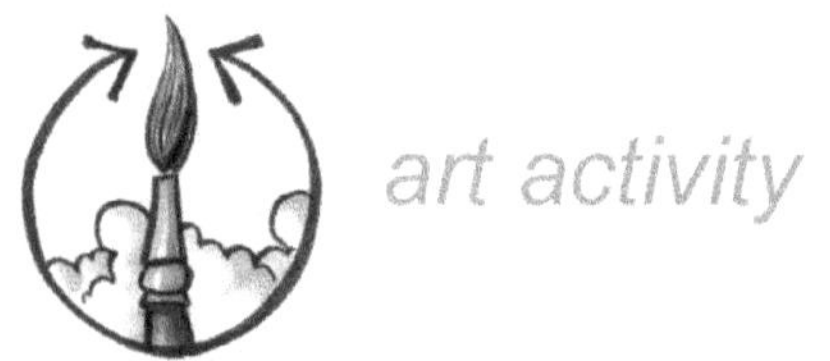

Scavenger Hunt Rubbings: A Texture Collage

Background: In this project, you will create textures by making rubbings on paper from different surfaces. You will then use this patterned paper to create a collage.

Materials: Crayons or oil pastels, watercolors, thin paper, glue, and scissors.

Directions:

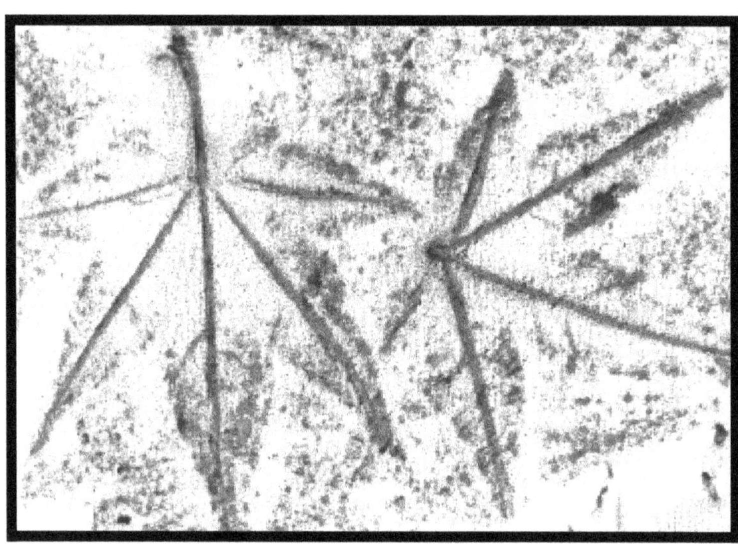

- Go on a scavenger hunt for textures to use to make your rubbings. To make a rubbing, lay your paper flat on a textured surface. Peel the wrapper off a crayon, and lay the crayon on its side. Rake the crayon across the surface of the paper to pick up the relief of the textures underneath. Try the surface of rocks, the bark of trees, the side of a basket, the bottom of your shoe, leaves on the sidewalk, and all of the other fascinating surfaces you encounter.

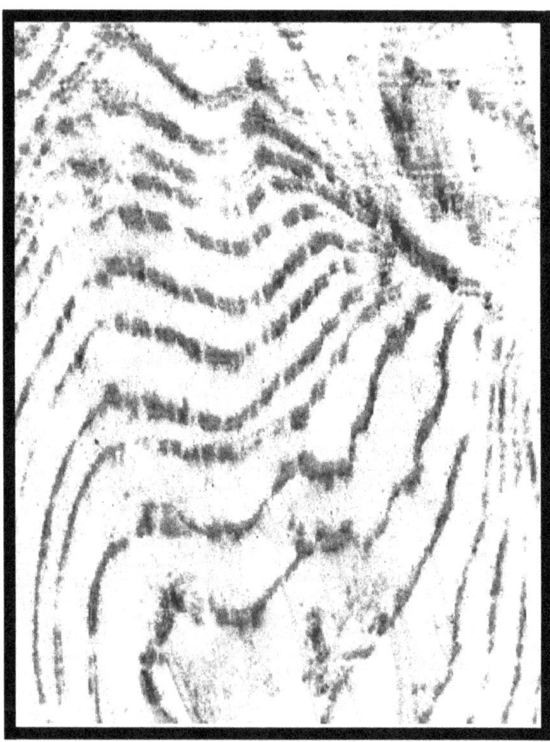

- Can you guess what was used to make the rubbings on this page? The answers are at the bottom of the next page.

- Use a variety of colors and fill several sheets of paper with unusual textures.

- You can paint with watercolors over the top of your rubbings to add background colors. This is because oil and water do not mix. The parts of the paper with crayon will repel the color. Try using contrasting colors for an exciting effect, such as blue with orange, green with red, or violet with yellow.

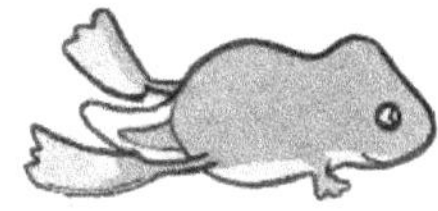

Using the image on page 57, trace the shapes onto your pieces of paper. You can use a sunny window to help you see through the paper. Cut out the shapes and glue them into all of the spaces of the drawing to fill it with color and texture.

Now use the rest of the rubbings to make an image of your own design.

Consider This: Which types of surfaces do you think made the most interesting rubbings: natural ones or man-made ones? Why?

____

____

From left to right, top to bottom: maple leaves, block letters, wicker chair, fence board, woven floor mat, sandstone

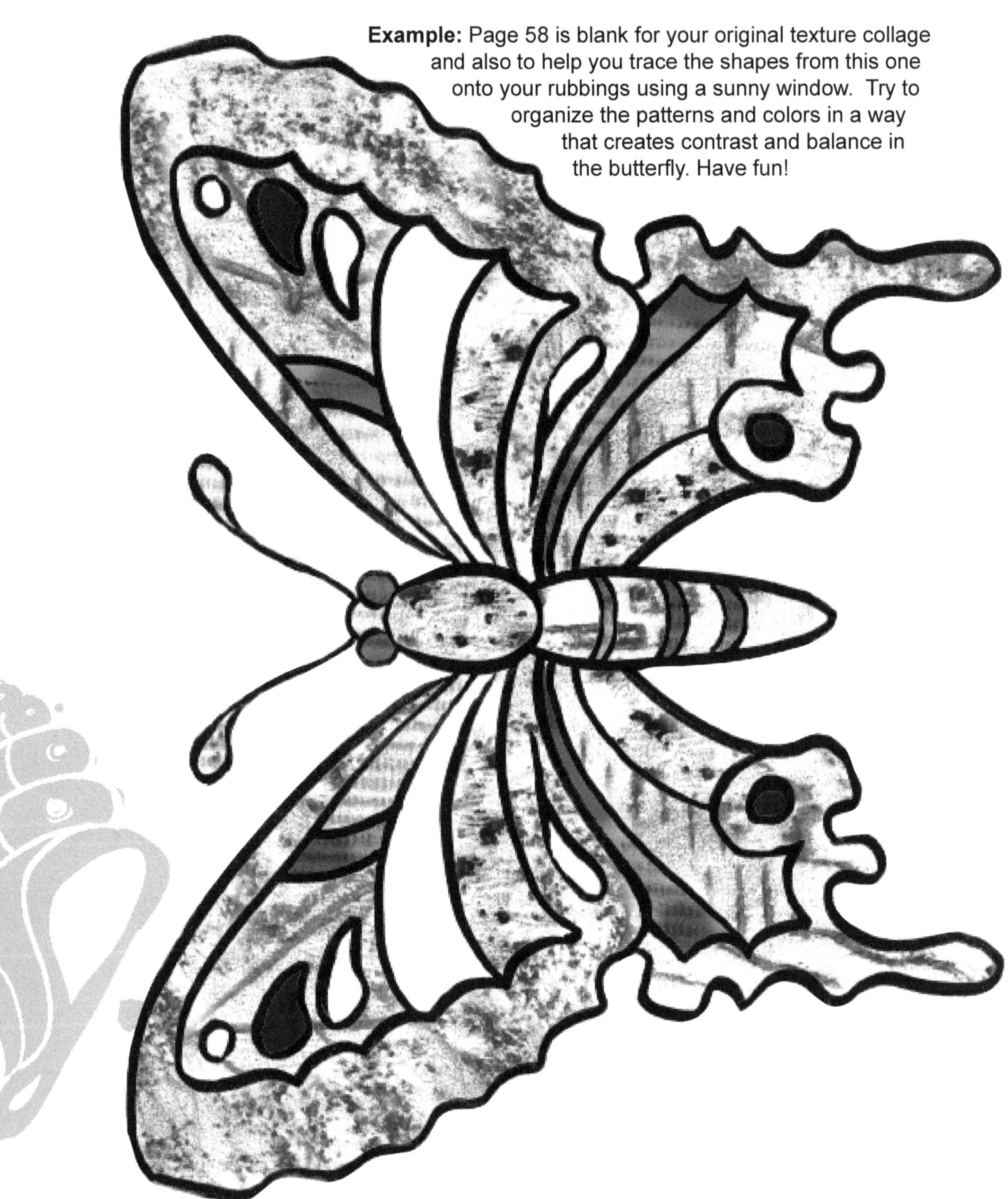

Example: Page 58 is blank for your original texture collage and also to help you trace the shapes from this one onto your rubbings using a sunny window. Try to organize the patterns and colors in a way that creates contrast and balance in the butterfly. Have fun!

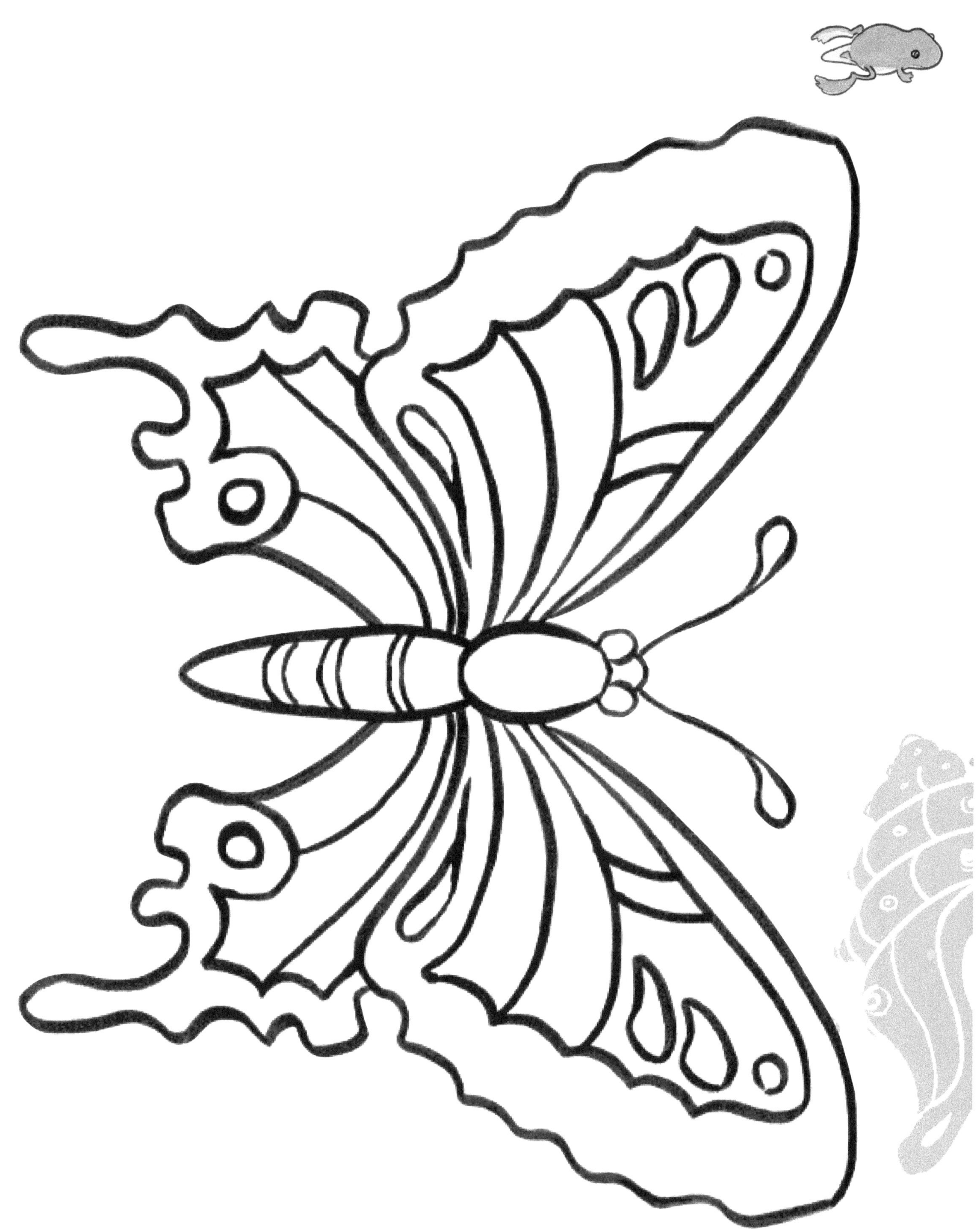

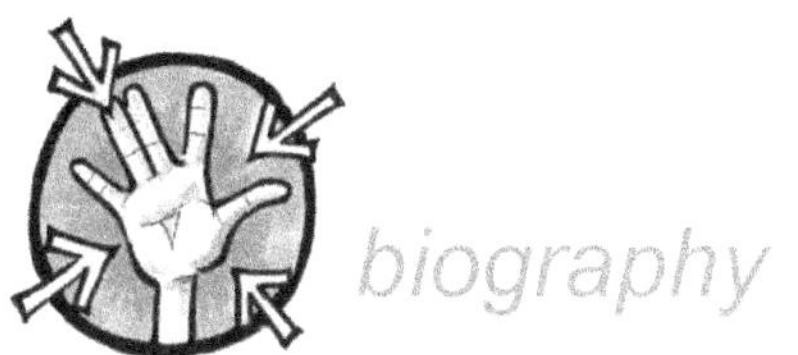

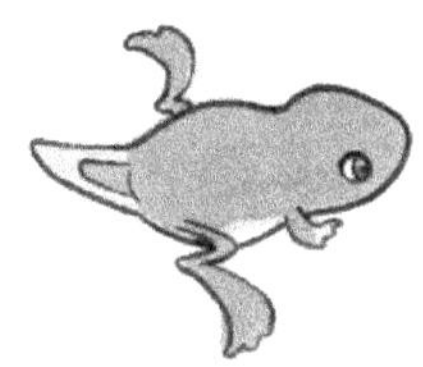

Focus on Andy Goldsworthy

Andy Goldsworthy is a very interesting sculptor who lives in Scotland. He never needs to go to the art store for supplies, and after he makes his art, he knows that it will break and disappear some day soon. Still, he works for hours and hours making his art. In the end, the only thing he has to show for his sculpture work is a photograph.

Andy Goldsworthy starts his artwork by getting up early in the morning and going on a walk. He looks closely at nature and tries to make all of his art out of things he finds in the wild. Sometimes, he stacks stones in beautiful, balanced towers. Sometimes, he gathers leaves from the forest floor and sorts them by color to lay them out in a spectacular design. In the winter, he might make beautiful sculptures completely out of icicles. He never uses string or glue, but rather only uses materials that he finds on his walk. He even stitches things together with thorns or freezes them with ice.

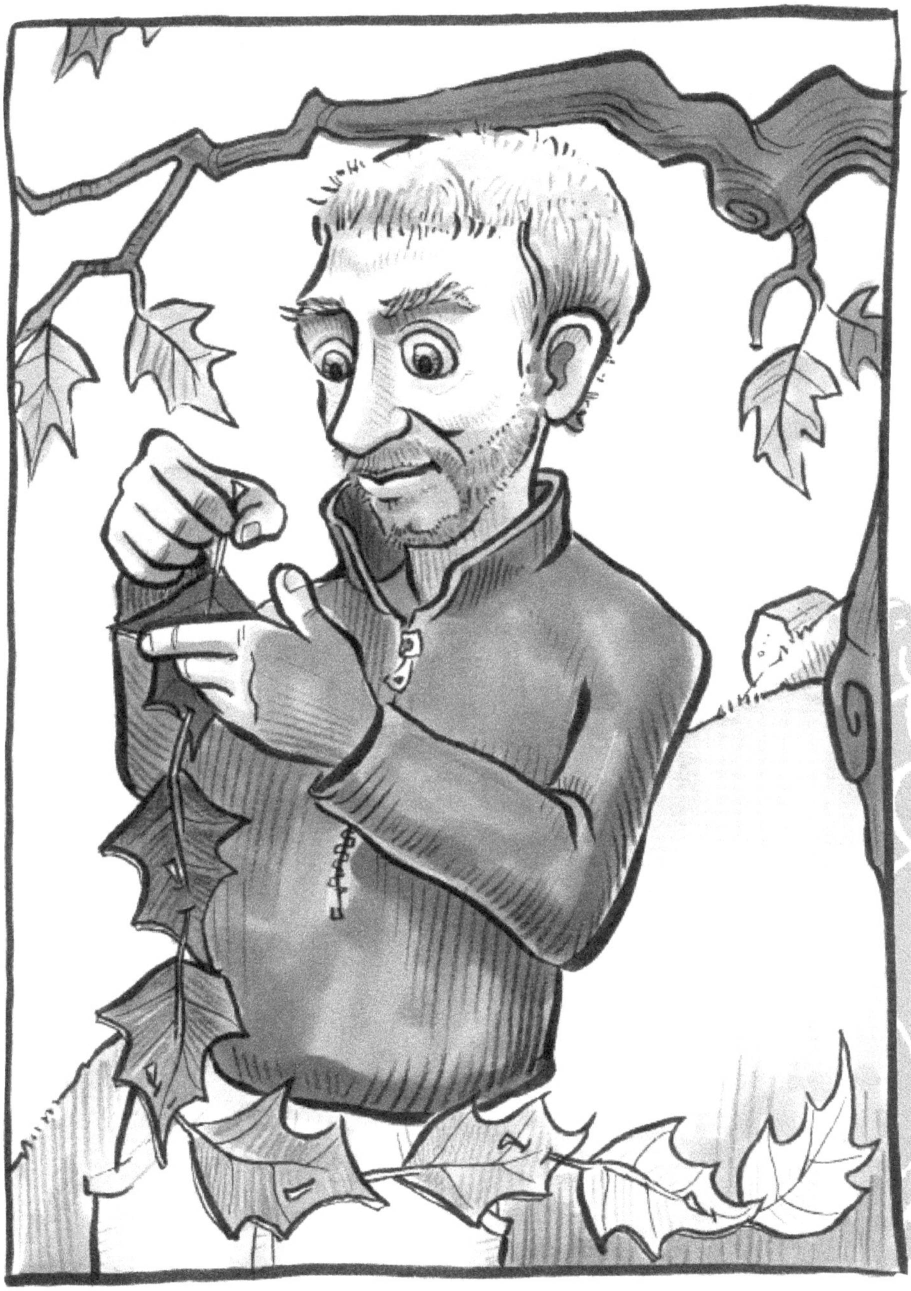

Andy Goldsworthy appreciates the idea that his artwork is made of natural materials and that, like nature, they will decompose and change. The forces of the wind, the sun, the seasons and the tides break his artwork, but at the same time, those forces created the conditions for his art to exist in the first place.

Exploration: Search the Web for images of Andy Goldsworthy's work. Better yet, go to the library and check out one of his books. Find one sculpture that is your favorite and answer the following questions:

What do you like about this artwork?

____

____

____

____

How do you imagine that it was made? What was the process like?

____

____

____

____

What do you think he might have seen on the day that he made the sculpture?

____

____

____

____

How long will it last? What do you think will cause it to fall apart?

____

____

____

____

Activity: Now go for a walk in the closest wild space to your house, and try to create a natural work of art inspired by Andy Goldsworthy. Remember that you don't want to do anything that will be permanent or harm the plants or trees. Take a camera along to record your sculpture or make a drawing of it. Write a short poem about your experience.

Going Further: Rent Andy Goldsworthy's film, "Rivers and Tides," so you can see the artist in action as he creates art in the Scottish countryside.

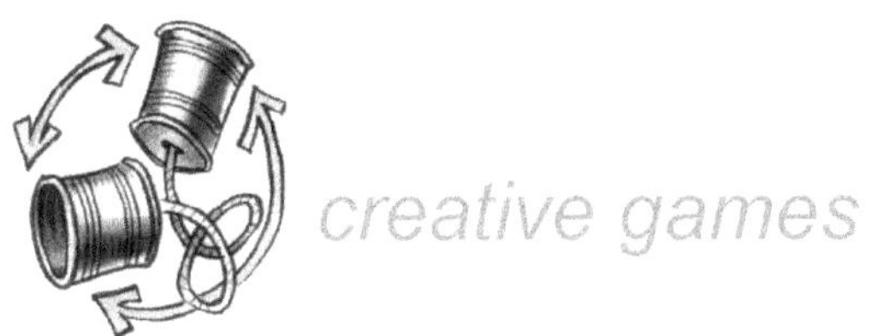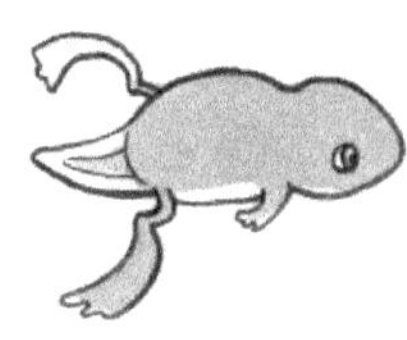

Tumbling Towers: A Balancing Game

Background: A stack of rocks is called a cairn. Traditionally, cairns are used as markers in rough terrain to show hikers where the trail goes. After you and a friend finish playing this game, you will leave several cairns behind for others to enjoy. This is a game that starts off as a contest, but ends up as an artwork. It is played outdoors, anywhere you find yourself surrounded by lots of rocks.

Materials: Lots of rocks, two players

Directions:

- The two players play "rock, paper, scissors" to determine who goes first. The person who is first finds a nice large rock to be the base rock and starts the game.

- The second player finds the biggest, flattest rock she can. Carefully, she balances it upon the first rock.

- The players continue to take turns, selecting smaller and smaller rocks and balancing them on top of the stack.

- After a few turns, the tower of stones will begin to wobble.

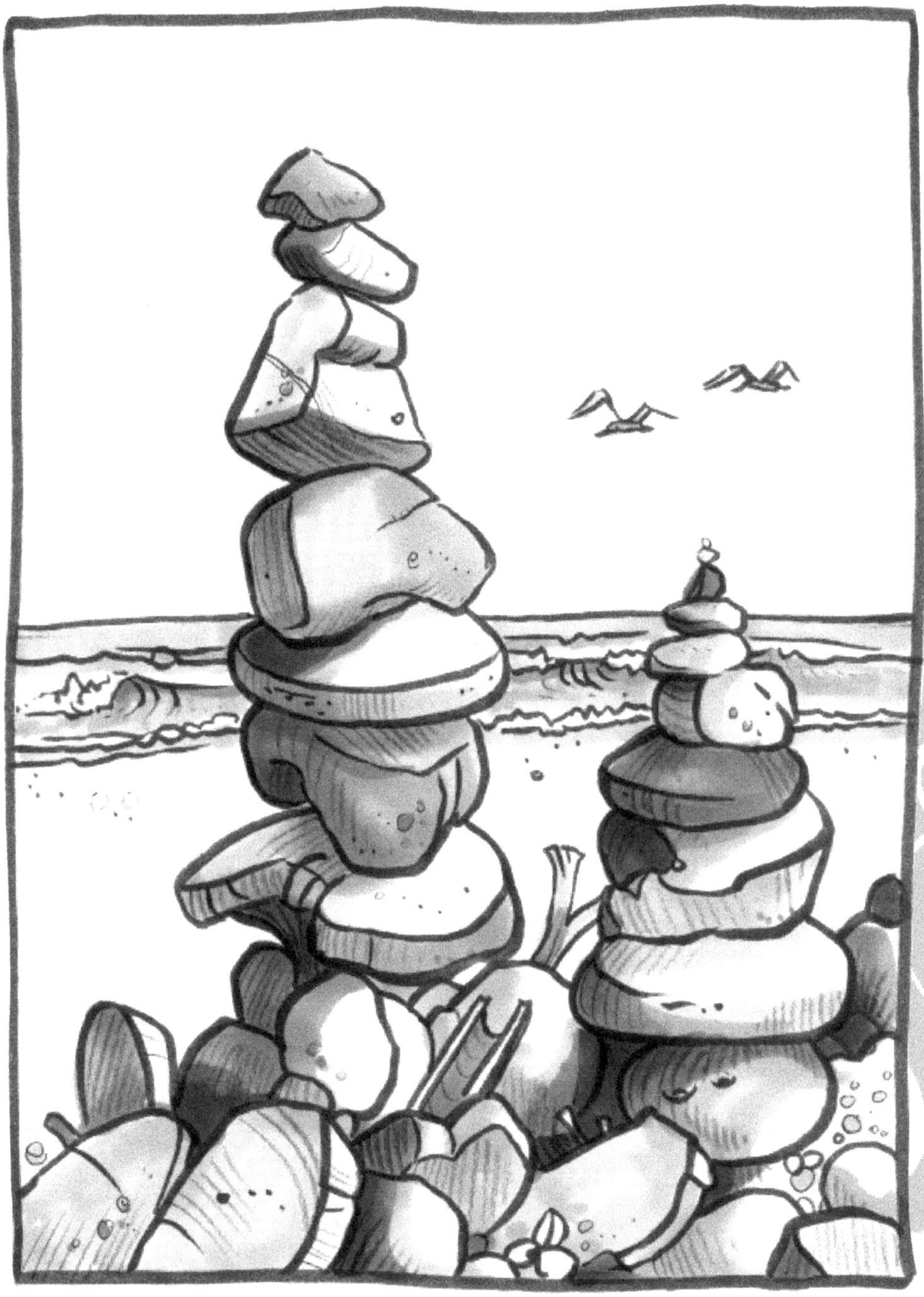

- The loser is the person who places the stone that makes the tower fall. But really, if you are outdoors, listening to birds and playing with rocks, are there any losers?

- After the tower topples, the two work together to get it back to the level where it was last. Then, they leave that tower standing and start a new game nearby.

- After a few rounds are played, the landscape is decorated in beautifully balanced cairns. Take a camera and shoot a picture of the cairns as the setting sun casts long shadows behind them.

Going Further: If you want a real challenge, build two cairns side by side and try to connect them together to create a natural stone arch. One way of doing this is to pile up some rocks between the cairns to support the arch as you build it and then carefully remove those support rocks after the arch is balanced.

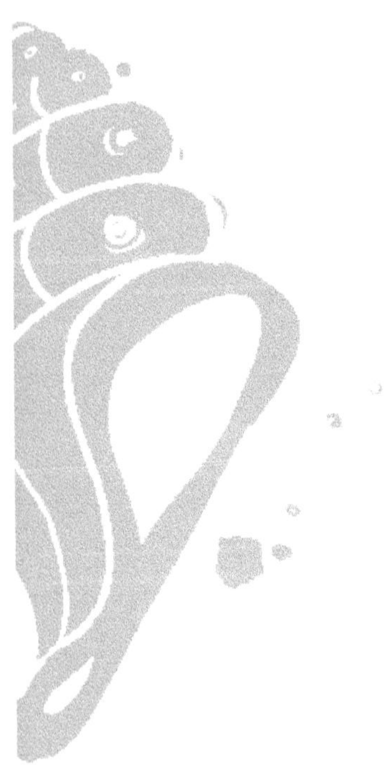

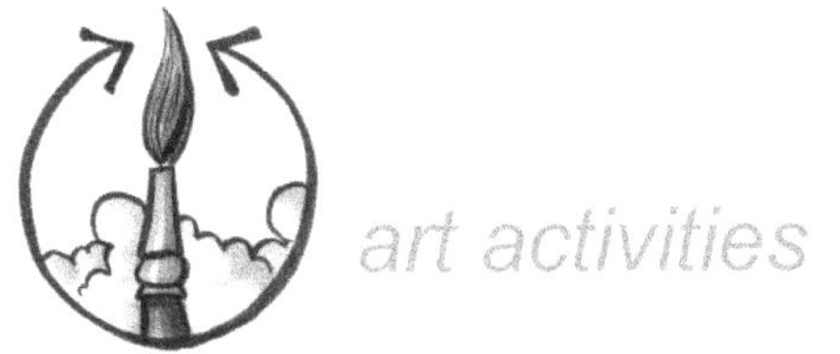 *art activities*

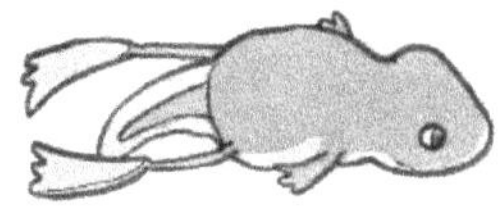

Tessellations and Connections

Background: Tessellations are geometric patterns that fit together perfectly without leaving any gaps. The squares on a checkerboard are a simple tessellation.

Tessellations are a good metaphor for nature: a system where every piece fits together, and there is no wasted space. In this project, you will be challenged to make your own tessellations.

Consider This: Think of some of the brilliant connections found in nature. Consider the food web and the ways that living things eat other living things in a big balancing act. We all depend upon each other for food.

For Example: Think of the way air is recycled: We exhale carbon dioxide and inhale oxygen. Plants do the opposite, and together, we recycle these gasses. Connections help create the beautiful balance we find in nature.

What is a connection that you have noticed in the natural world?

____

____

____

____

Materials: Paper, scissors, pencil, coloring tools, tape

Directions:
- To create your tessellation, make a small piece of paper about 2 inches square. Starting on one edge of the paper, draw a shape that makes you think of a natural form. Maybe you will draw a leaf edge, shark's tooth, lobster claw, or spiral.

1

2

❧ Carefully cut this shape out. If it is really detailed, you could use an X-Acto knife.

❧ Slide the shape in a straight line to the opposite edge of the square and tape it on. See illustration. Now, if you had several of these new shapes, you could interlock them and line them up like train cars.

❧ You are going to repeat steps 1-3 from the top edge and slide the cut shape down to the bottom, taping it on.

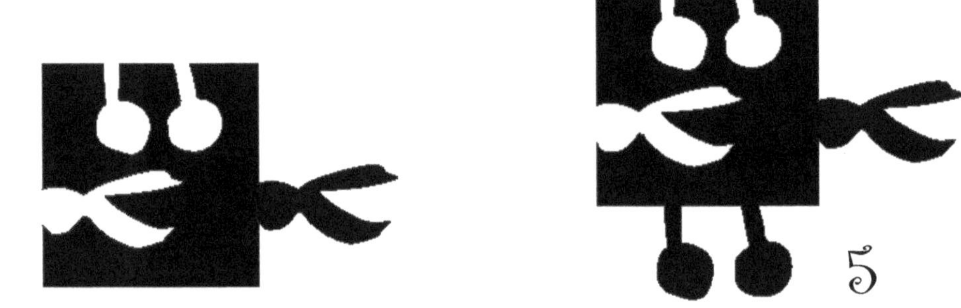

❧ You can cut holes out of your stencil in any shape you would like.

❧ Using your final shape as a stencil, trace it on a piece of paper.

❧ Lift it and place it next to this pencil tracing so that they fit together, and trace again. Fill the paper with these shapes.

❧ You can color your design in many ways. One way is to color every other square as though it were a checkerboard. Then it looks like black shapes on a white background. When you blink your eyes, it will shift and look like white shapes on a black background. You could also color your shapes if you wanted.

Going Further: Can you create a tessellation made of shapes that resemble a specific animal? Go on the Web and find images of some of the tessellations made by M.C. Escher.

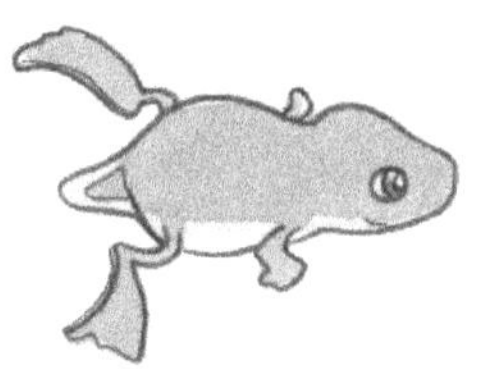

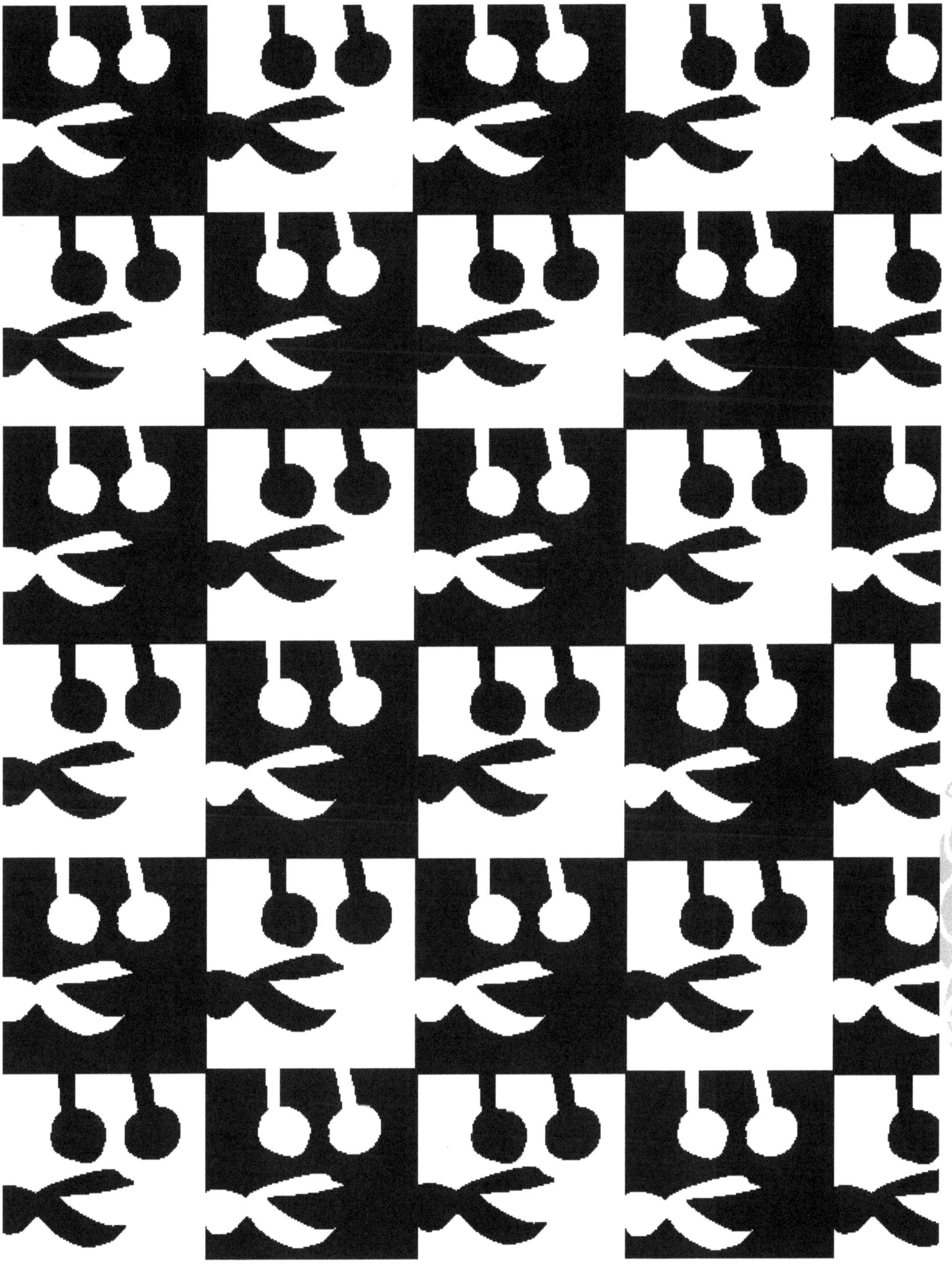

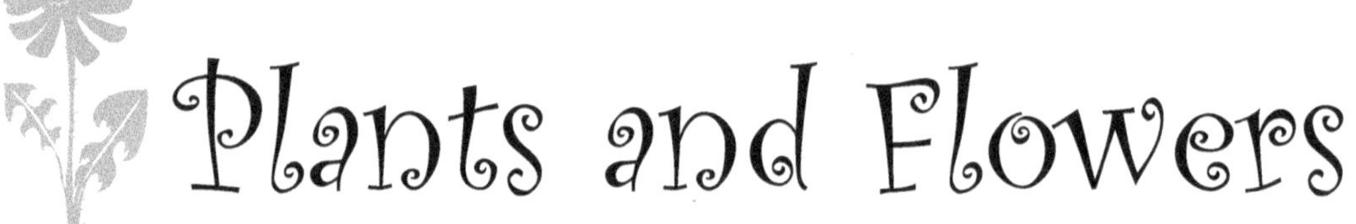

Plants and Flowers

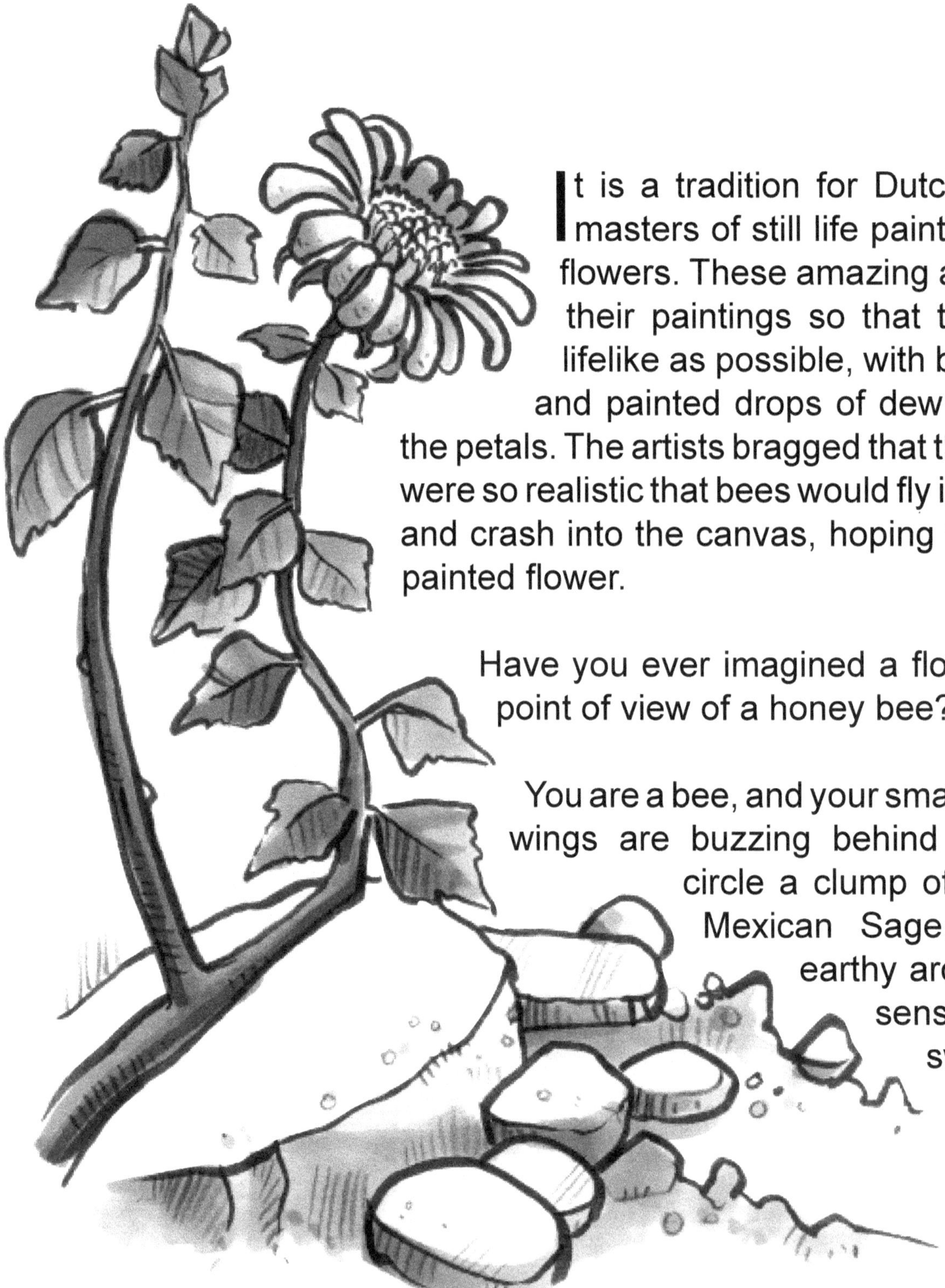

It is a tradition for Dutch artists, the masters of still life paintings, to paint flowers. These amazing artists crafted their paintings so that they were as lifelike as possible, with brilliant colors and painted drops of dew sparkling on the petals. The artists bragged that their paintings were so realistic that bees would fly into the studio and crash into the canvas, hoping to pollinate a painted flower.

Have you ever imagined a flower from the point of view of a honey bee?

You are a bee, and your small transparent wings are buzzing behind you as you circle a clump of bright violet Mexican Sage. Its smoky, earthy aroma fills your senses, and you swoop down to one of

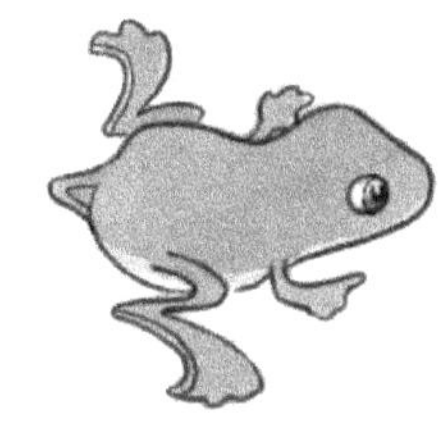

3

its flowers for a closer look. You realize that the flower is covered in a carpet of purple velvet. You climb inside an inviting tunnel into the oblong flower and see a smooth, white, shady oasis. You take a sweet sip of sage nectar. Just as you drink, you feel a tap on your furry back as an enormous stamen pops down and dusts you with pollen so that you will pollinate other flowers as you pursue more nectar on other plants.

In this chapter, we will be exploring wild plants and looking closely at the design of their flowers, the changes they go through with the seasons, and their relationships to other organisms. Perhaps you will draw a flower with enough care that you fool the ultimate art critic, the common honey bee.

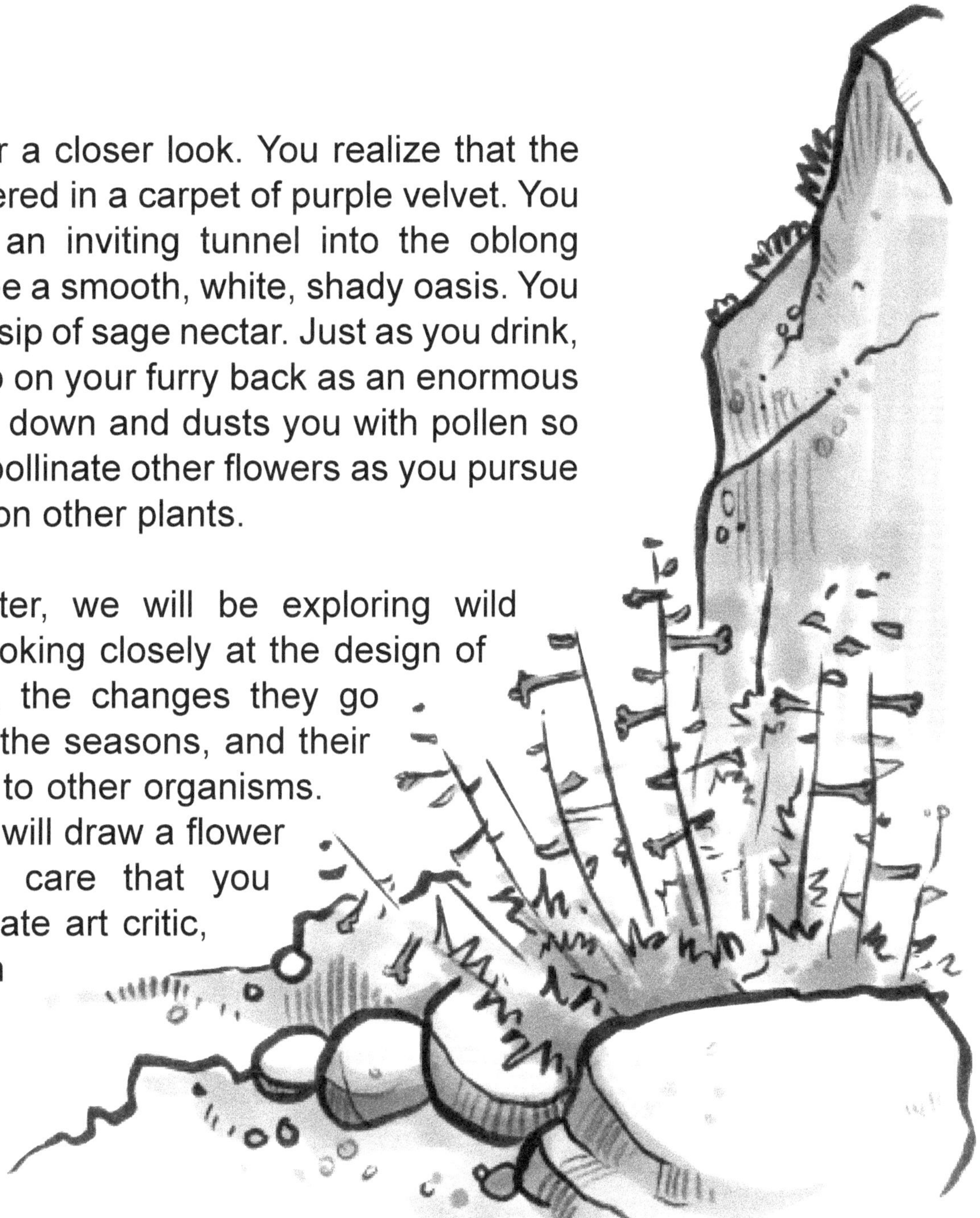

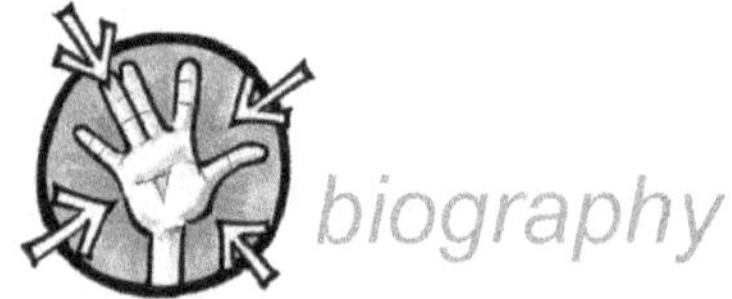

Focus on Beatrix Potter

Beatrix Potter was born in London, England, in 1866. She is best known for writing and illustrating "The Tale of Peter Rabbit." This is a timeless story about a curious young rabbit who barely escapes from a grumpy farmer's vegetable patch. The drawings in the tale are very realistic, with true-to-life rabbits and plants. They are created with watercolors and show Potter's experience as a naturalist artist.

As a child of strict, wealthy parents, Potter did not have the opportunity to play with other children very often, so she would occupy her time drawing, writing and exploring the wilds near her home. She kept a number of unusual pets, including frogs, ferrets, newts, and, of course, rabbits.

Beatrix Potter was an avid naturalist. She was most noted as a mycologist, a scientist who studies mushrooms. She made detailed watercolors of various types of fungus and lichens. She studied the ways that mushrooms reproduce using spores. She would draw the spores, which are very small, while looking through a microscope.

Her career as a children's book author and illustrator took a while to get started. She had a very difficult time getting "The Tale of Peter Rabbit" published. Eventually, she found a publisher who loved the book and asked her to illustrate it again in color. She fell in love with and married her publisher.

Beatrix Potter was an avid conservationist. She saw that tourism and development were beginning to harm the Lake District that she so loved as a child and artist. When she died, she left all of the land her family had owned to the National Trust so that it would be protected as a nature preserve.

Exploration: Search the Internet and find some images of Beatrix Potter's artwork. What aspects of her work let you know that she spent a lot of time studying nature?

____

____

____

Going Further: Can you find examples of her drawings of fungus and lichens? How are these drawings like the ones in her children's books? How are they different?

____

____

____

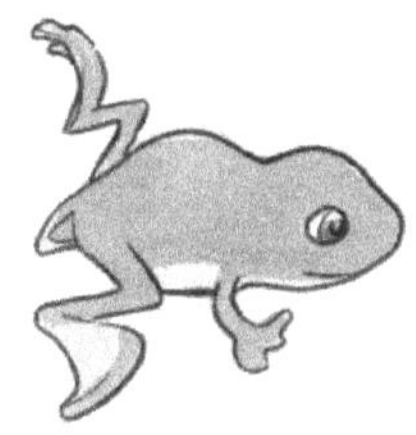

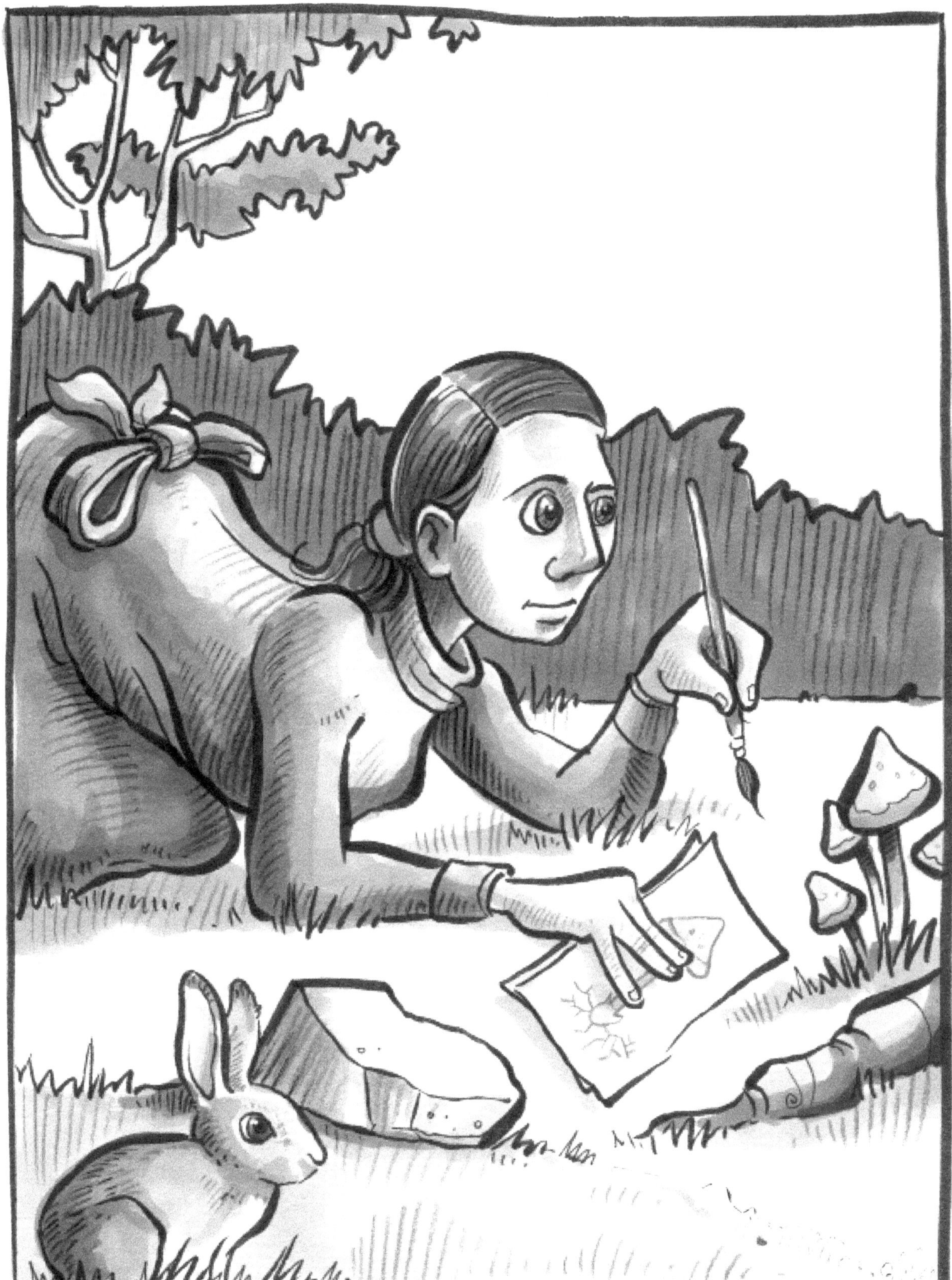

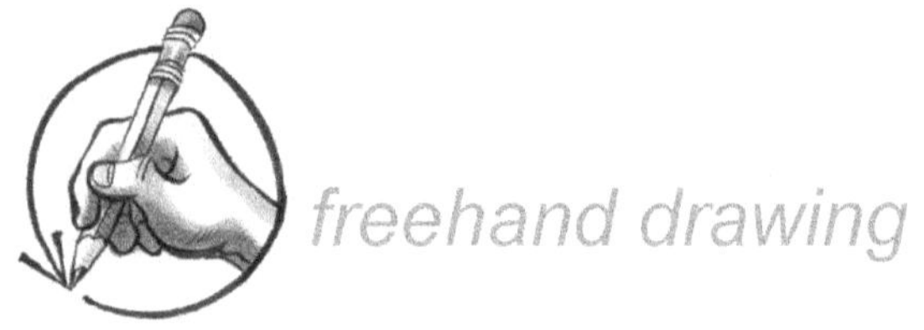

Botanical Illustration

Background: This is your opportunity to be a naturalist explorer. Walk into your backyard pretending that you are an explorer lost deep in the Amazon rain forest. You have just discovered a rare, unidentified plant specimen. You will now try to draw it in detail, roots and all, to share with people back home, because your actual plant will wilt and fade before you have the time to trek it back to civilization.

Materials: Watercolors, a black pen with waterproof ink, and pencil.
Tip: You can test your pen to find out if it has waterproof ink by drawing a line on paper, letting it dry, and trying to smear the line with water.

Directions:

- Find a plant that is partly in flower. If possible, gently dig near a small part of your plant so that you can see what the roots look like. You can use a bottle of water to rinse off the soil and help you see the roots' color.

- Lightly in pencil, sketch out the entire plant. There is a space for you at the end of the lessonon page 74.

- Pay particular attention to the flowers. Naturalist artists often like to draw the flowers in several stages — as buds, flowers and seed pods — to show the process of flowering. Sometimes, you can see these stages all at once on different parts of a plant. Look carefully from flower to flower to see which ones you think are newer and which are older. You can dissect a flower, pulling it apart so that you can see and count the parts that are out of view.

- Can you identify the parts on your flower that are illustrated in the diagram above? The parts include the stamen, pistil, sepal and petal. As you draw, carefully count the parts of your flower. Fill in the chart on the page 73. These numbers help botanists determine what family a flower belongs to.

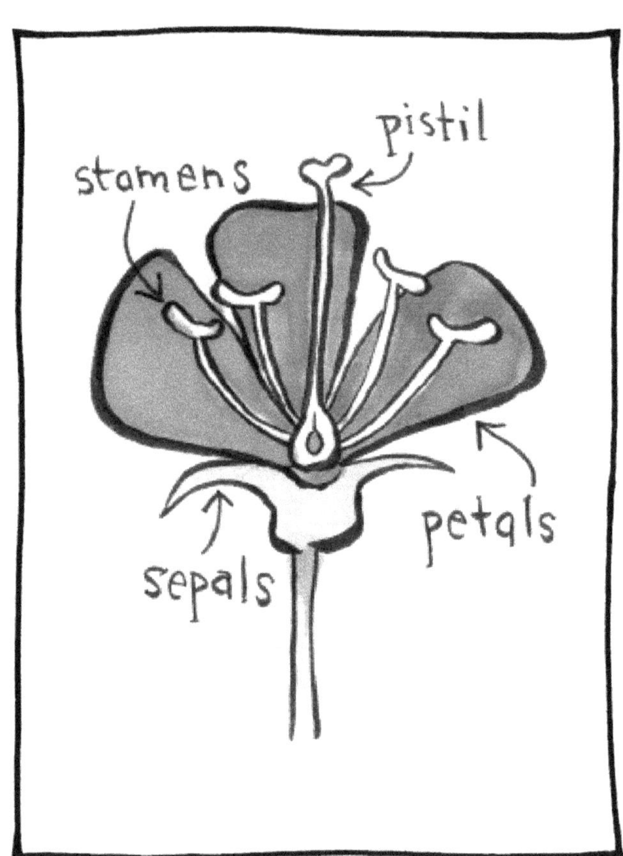

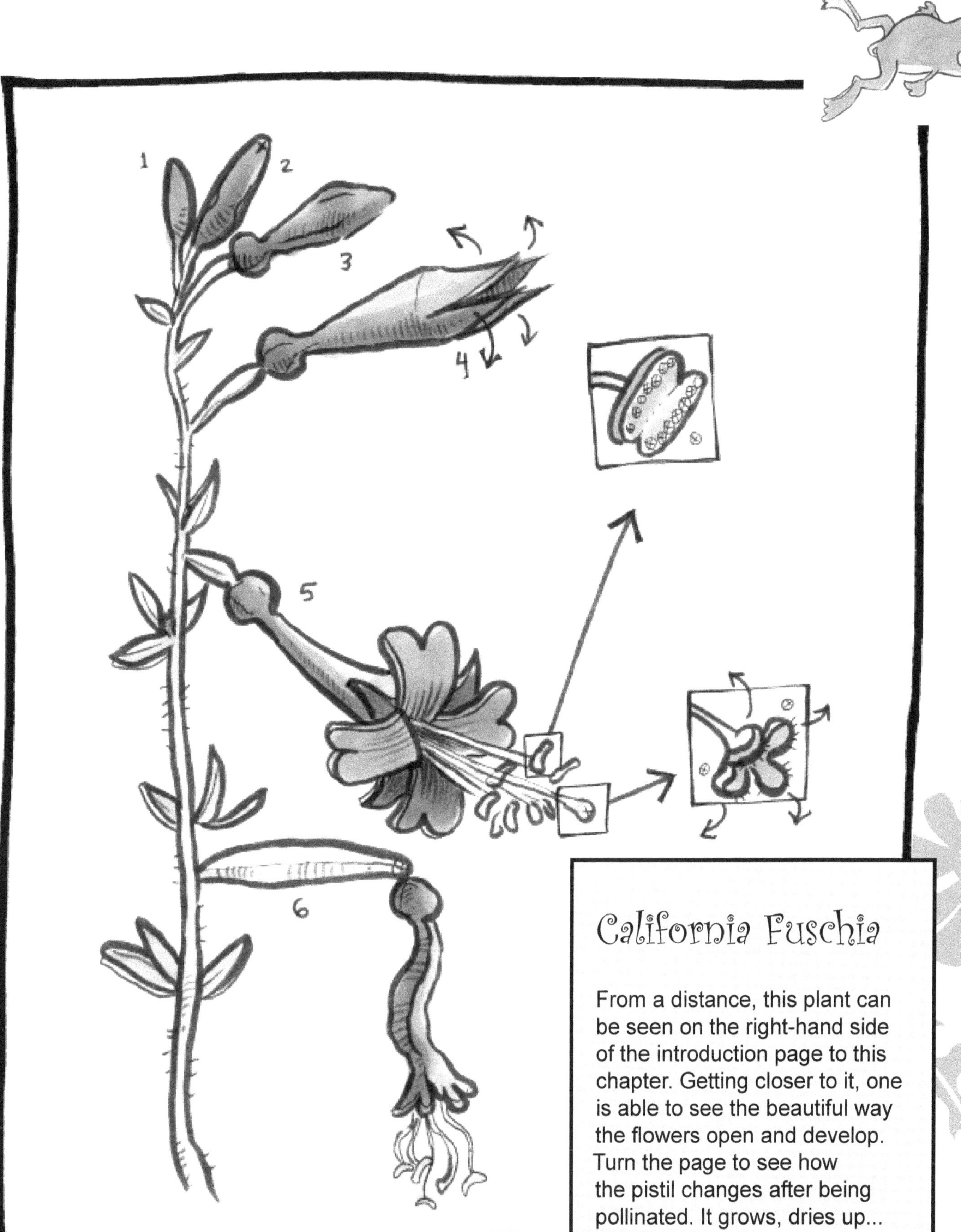

California Fuschia

From a distance, this plant can be seen on the right-hand side of the introduction page to this chapter. Getting closer to it, one is able to see the beautiful way the flowers open and develop. Turn the page to see how the pistil changes after being pollinated. It grows, dries up...

... and splits open in four directions. Then, with little parachutes of cotton, the seeds drop to the ground to wait for the rain and start over. At certain times of the year, you can see all of these stages at once on this plant. Every plant has its own unique way of reproducing. Study yours closely.

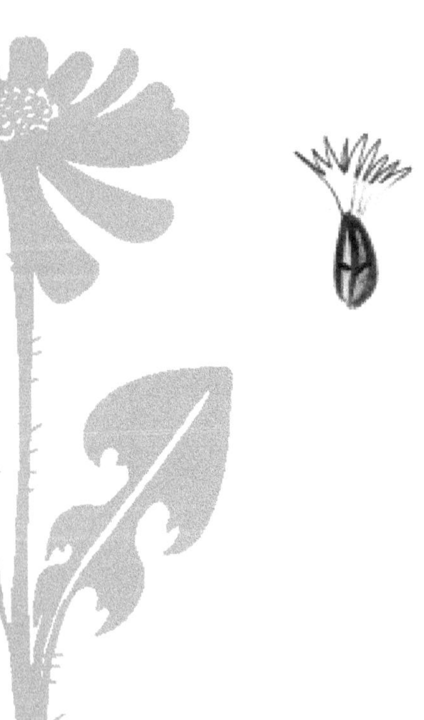

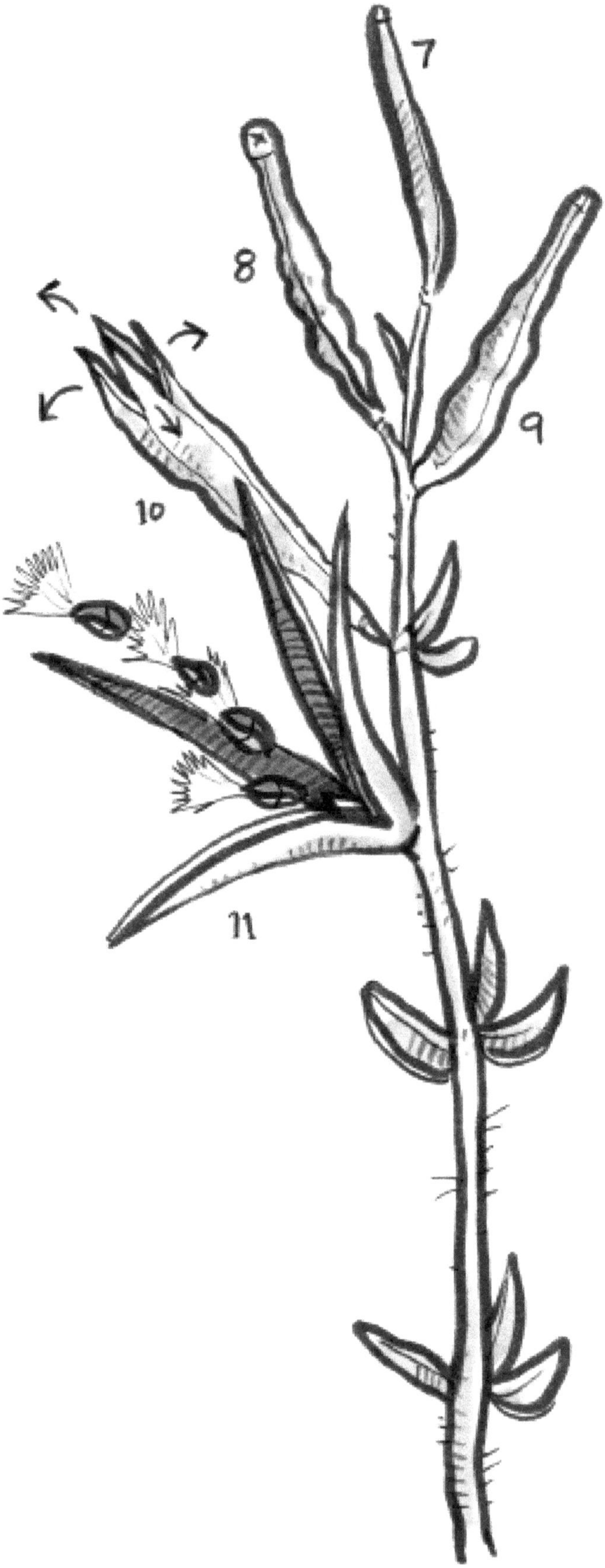

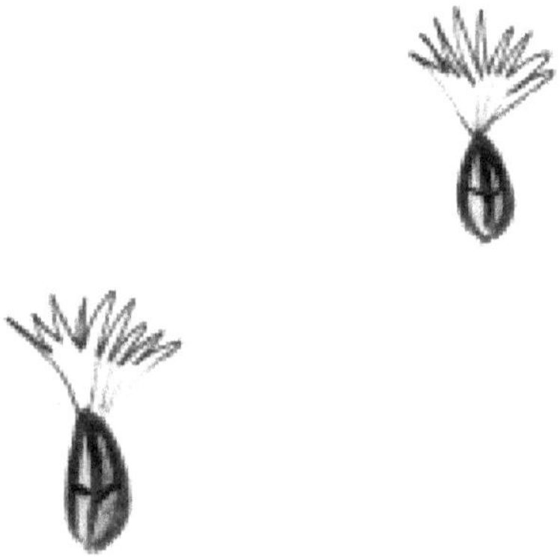

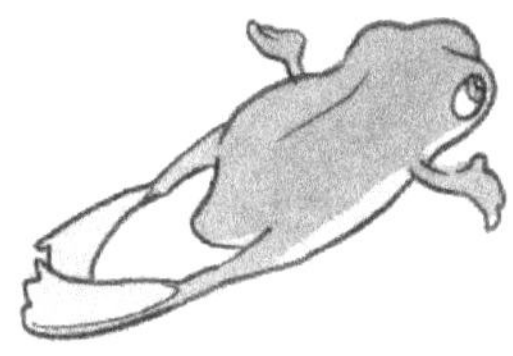

꣠ Use the waterproof pen to carefully outline your drawing. Then, lightly erase the remaining pencil marks.

꣠ Using the watercolors, begin to add color. If your brush is too wet, it can wrinkle your paper. It is helpful to keep a paper towel in your hand so that you can blot your brush and control the amount of paint that it holds.

꣠ Show your drawing to a family member or friend, and challenge them to find the location outside where you drew it.

Going Further: See if you can identify your plant using a book, such as a garden handbook or a field guide to local wild plants.

	How many are there?	Make a drawing of these parts ...
Petals		
Sepals		
Stamens		
Pistils		

plant name:

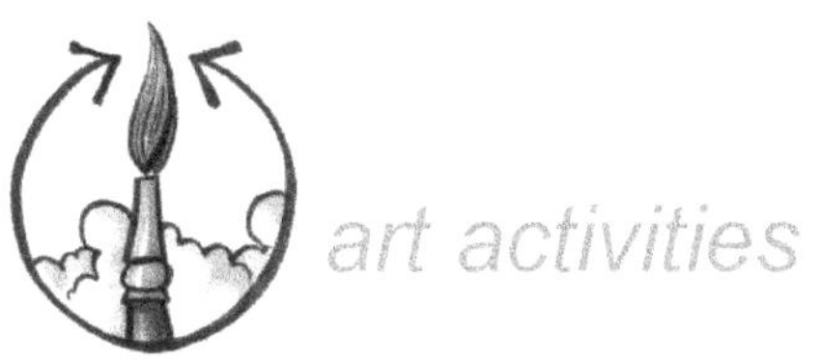

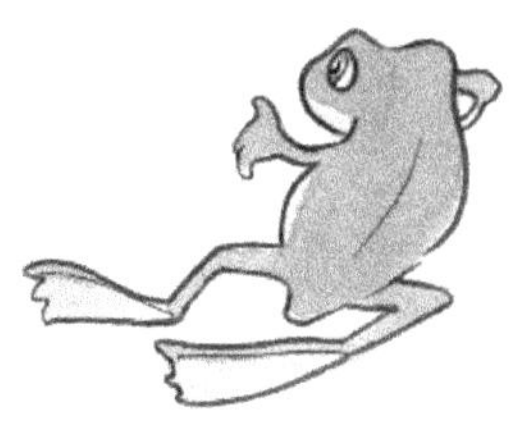

Making a Tree From a Stick

Background: Lines can have a lot of character. There is the clean, even line of a ballpoint pen. There is the grace of a line made by a brush, which changes in thickness throughout a stroke. However, for drawing the rough natural textures and shapes of an old tree, nothing beats a stick.

Materials: The biggest piece of paper or cardboard you can find — perhaps a piece of a large box that is intended to be recycled; India ink thinned slightly with water or black paint in a small yogurt container; a knife for changing the point on your stick.

Directions:

- Find a tree to draw. It might be a lonely oak in a wide, grassy field with heavy limbs and thick, chunky bark. Maybe it is a tall, noble redwood with soft, fern-like needles filtering the sunlight. Or, it could be a yellow aspen in autumn with leaves that sound like water in the wind.

- Find a good stick to use as a drawing tool. Ideally, you will find a thin stick about 3 or 4 feet long.

- Dip the stick in paint or ink to make your marks. Draw with your whole arm, not just your wrist. Try drawing one of your trees' leaves in the square on the next page.

- Lay your paper or cardboard on the ground between you and the tree. That way you will be able to stand back from your drawing and see the whole tree.

- Draw the tree from the ground up. Notice how the branches slowly get thinner as they move up from the trunk. First, draw the tree as though it has no leaves, to get the shape of the branches.

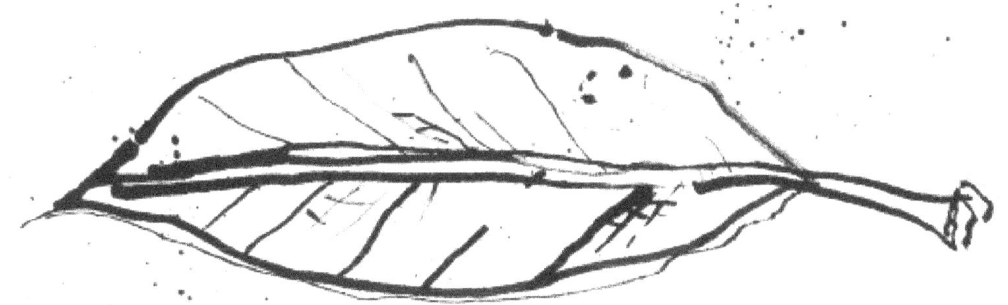

⚐ Try using different types of sticks for adding texture or shadows to the trunk. Look for signs of creatures that make their homes in your tree. You could include them in your drawing.

⚐ Look closely at the leaf shapes. Fill the branches with leaves. Consider creating the leaves using fossil prints from the next lesson.

⚐ After the ink dries on your painting, you can add color with crayons or chalk pastels. You might also use watercolors as long as the ink you used is waterproof.

Reflection: Hang your drawing in your room. It will always bring back memories of the day you spent outside making it. As time passes, visit your tree now and then to see what has changed since you drew it.

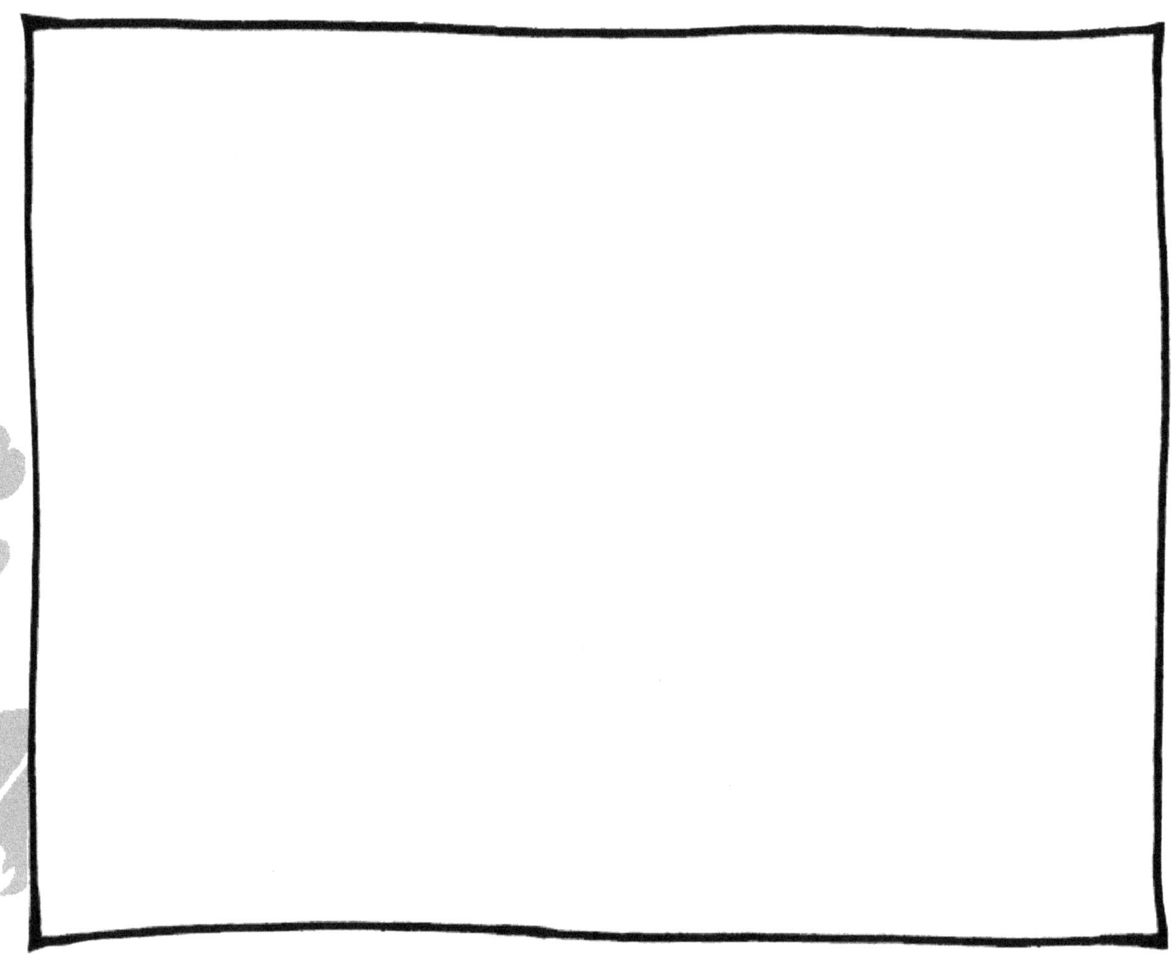

Your leaf goes in the space above. After you draw it, consider using the real leaf you drew it from as a bookmark in this book.

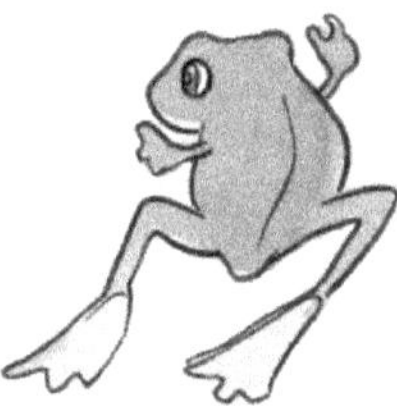

California Bay Laurel

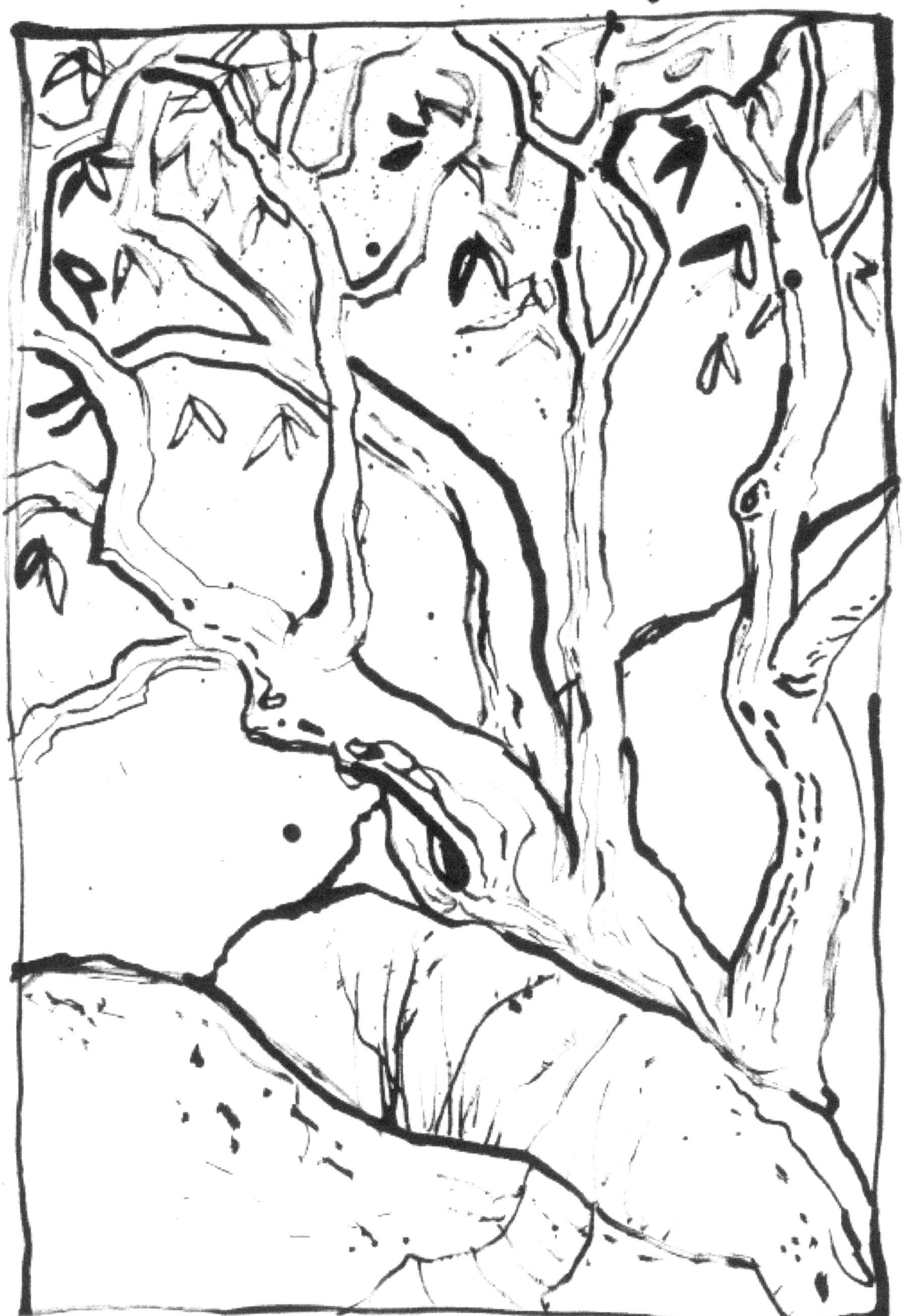

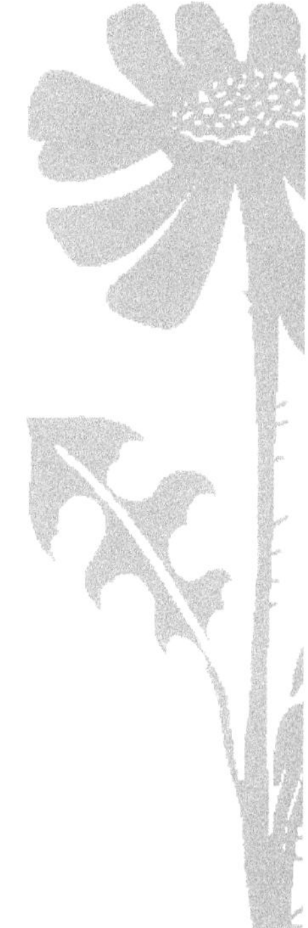

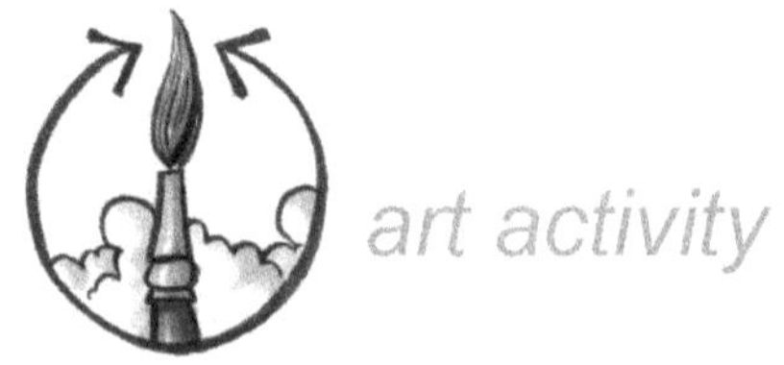

Fossil Prints

Background: Fossils are the impressions of plants or animals that have been captured in sandstone. These prints you will be making will look like fossils because they capture the relief of whatever natural object you make them from. In art, relief refers to the surface textures of an object. This is a very easy print making technique that is excellent for making cards and designs for friends.

Materials: Modeling clay, plastic knives or clay tools, stamp pads or a plate and thinned paint, found natural objects, colored paper

Directions:

◁ Go on a scavenger hunt for forms that will leave interesting impressions when pressed into clay. The veins on the backside of a leaf work really well. Ferns, seashells, pods, small pinecones and bark are also good choices.

◁ To flatten the clay, press it against a flat surface. Then press the object into the clay. You can trim the outside edges of the clay to give it an interesting shape.

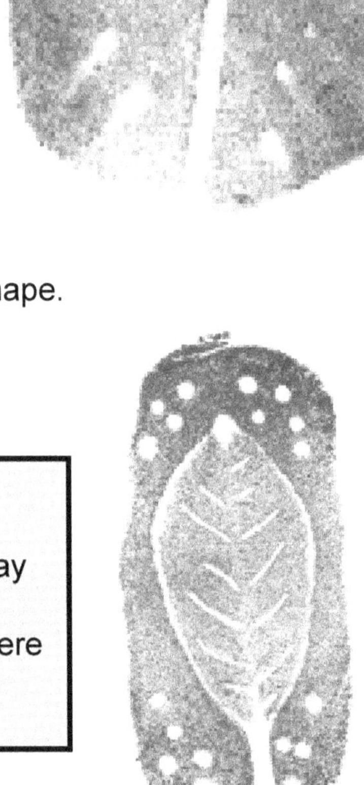

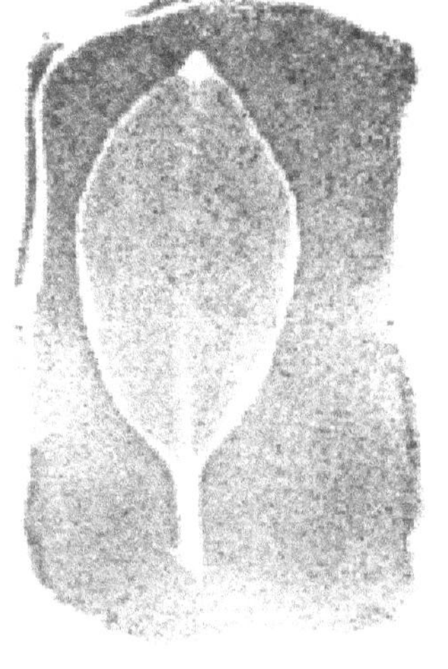

The leaf on the left was simply pressed into the clay and printed. In the print to the right, dots and lines were added with a sharp twig.

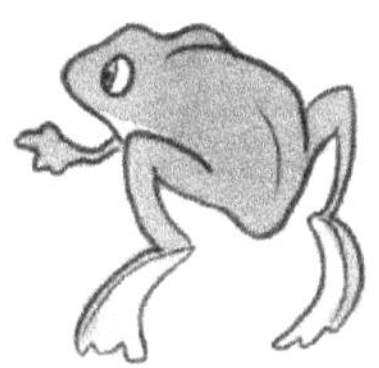

Ink the clay with a stamp pad, and then print. Consider using scratch paper for your first printings until you get the hang of it. If you don't press too hard and your clay is sturdy, you can usually get about ten good prints before the design starts to fill in.

Can you guess what natural objects were used to make the prints on this page? *Answers are on the next page.*

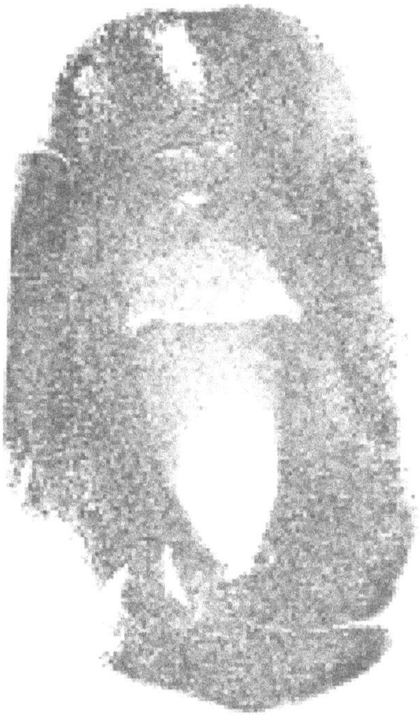

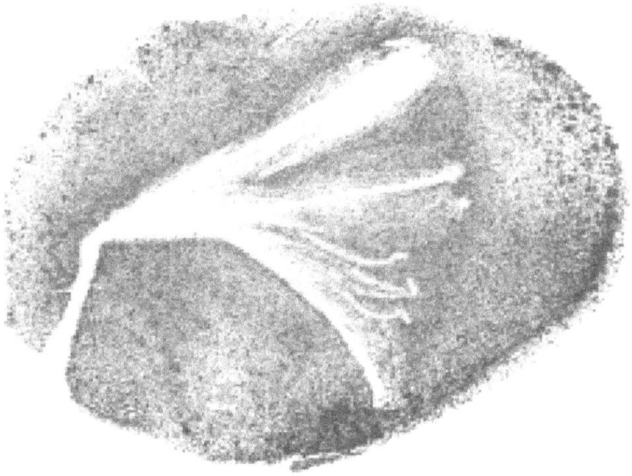

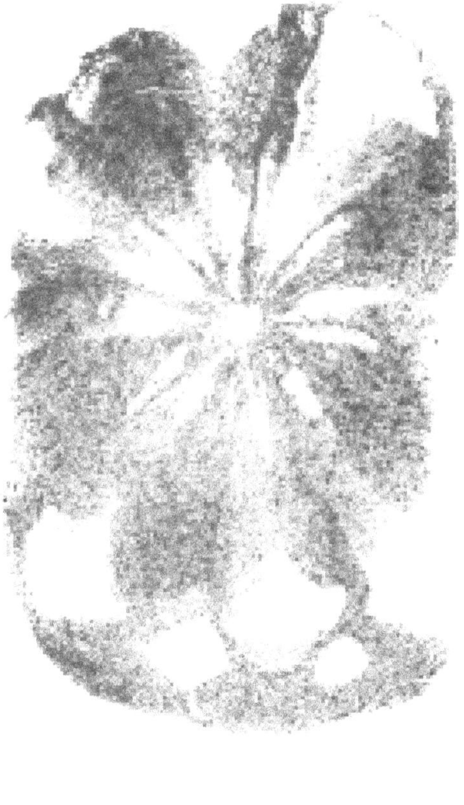

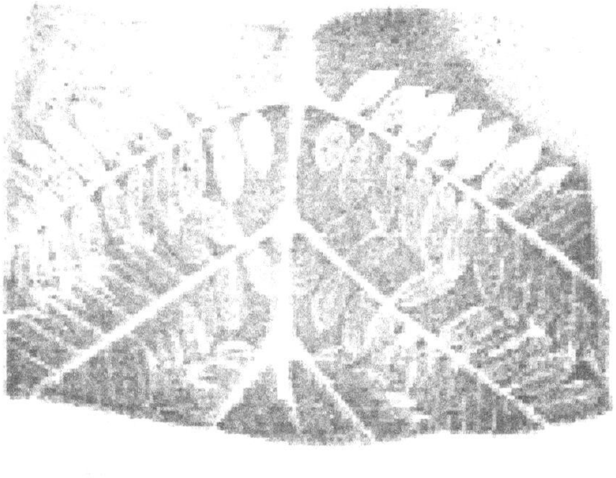

Going Further: You can also make designs by carving into your clay. This is called relief printing and was used commonly in Japan, where artists carved intricate designs out of pieces of wood. When you print your design on paper, the parts of the design that you carve away from your clay will be the color of the paper, and the rest will be the color of the ink. To begin, try carving out and printing your name.

What do you have to do to the letters to make this work?

____

____

____

Put some of your favorite prints in the squares below.

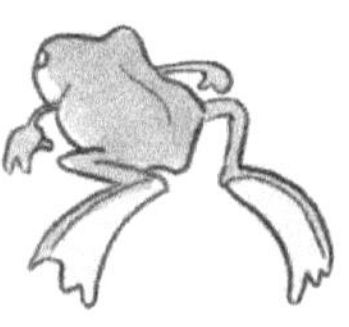

Focus on Katsushika Hokusai

Hokusai was a Japanese artist who was born in 1760. He was recognized as one of the greatest artists in all of Japan. Using a bamboo brush and hand-ground ink, Hokusai created whimsical drawings of people, landscapes, plants, birds and animals. He was a skilled woodblock printer and is most famous for his series of prints of views of Mount Fuji.

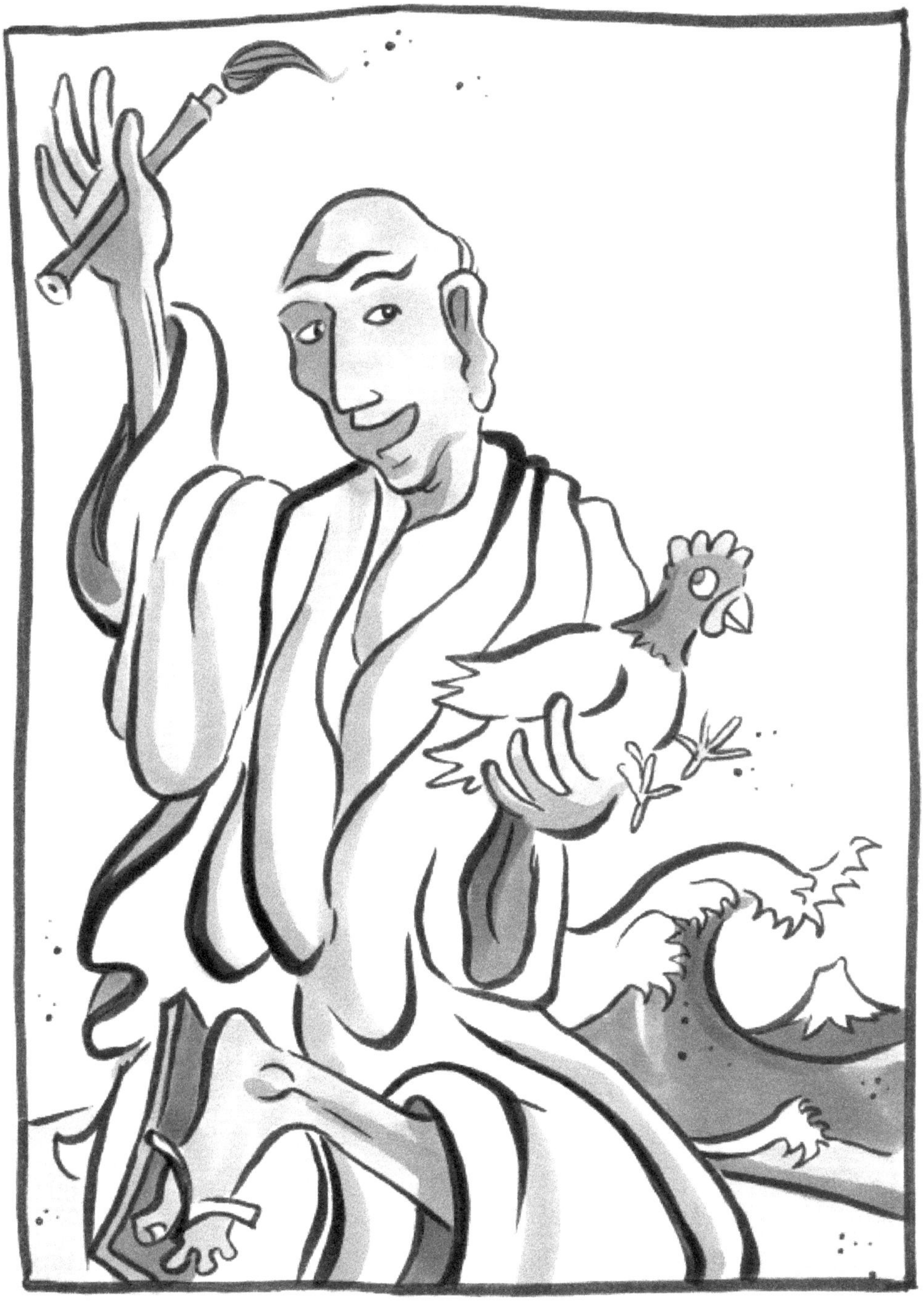

Hokusai was known for performing unusual artistic feats that challenged people's ideas of art. Once, he was invited to paint for the Shogun, the military leader of Japan. Hokusai is said to have unrolled a very large sheet of paper onto the floor before the leader. With a broom dipped in blue paint, he drew a graceful curve across the page. Then, he took a chicken, dipped its feet in red paint and let it run across the paper. As the audience looked upon in astonishment, Hokusai revealed that his painting was of red maple leaves floating down the Tatsuta River.

Hokusai was influenced by Taoism, which is a philosophy about the importance of honoring the balance and harmony found in nature.

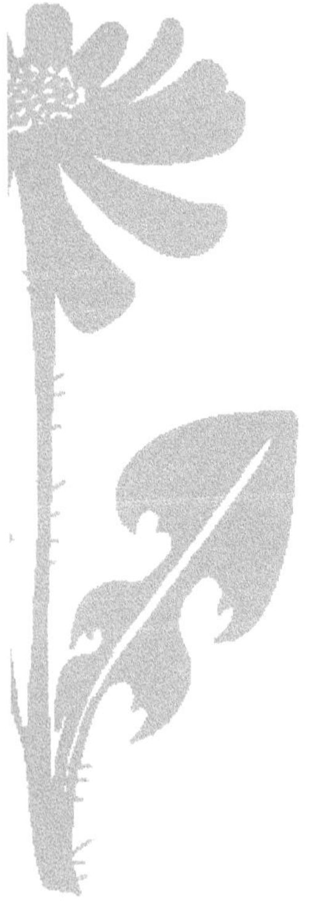

One symbol for this is the yin and yang symbol, which can be seen here. This symbol represents the balance of opposites in the world. Hokusai's paintings always had areas of detail and areas of emptiness to make them appear balanced and open.

Exploration: Search the Internet for an image of Hokusai's most famous image, "The Great Wave." Look closely at the detail to see the ways the texture of the water is drawn. There is a giant yin and yang symbol hidden in this painting. Can you see it? Why do you think that Hokusai painted the wave in this way? What might he be trying to say about the sea?

____

____

____

____

____

____

____

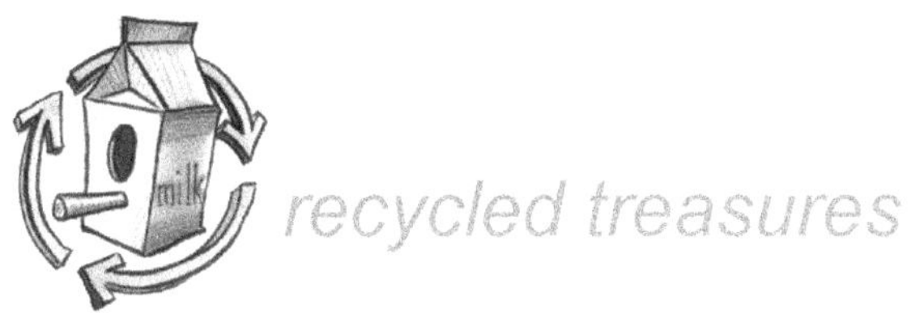
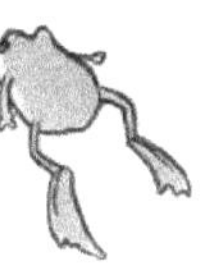

A Weed Garden

For Thought: What makes a plant a weed? ______________________________
____

Background: It is odd that many of the weeds that invade our lawns are actually some of the most useful plants we have around. We work really hard to get rid of them, but if we study them, we can learn to see that besides having their own beauty, they can offer us food and medicine.

Two common useful weeds are dandelions and plantain. People have eaten dandelion greens for thousands of years. They are very high in Vitamins A, C and iron. Plantain is a natural antibiotic that has been used for treating cuts and scrapes for just as long.

In this project, we are going to try to honor weeds and wild plants by making a garden of them. The challenge will be to use found objects as pots.

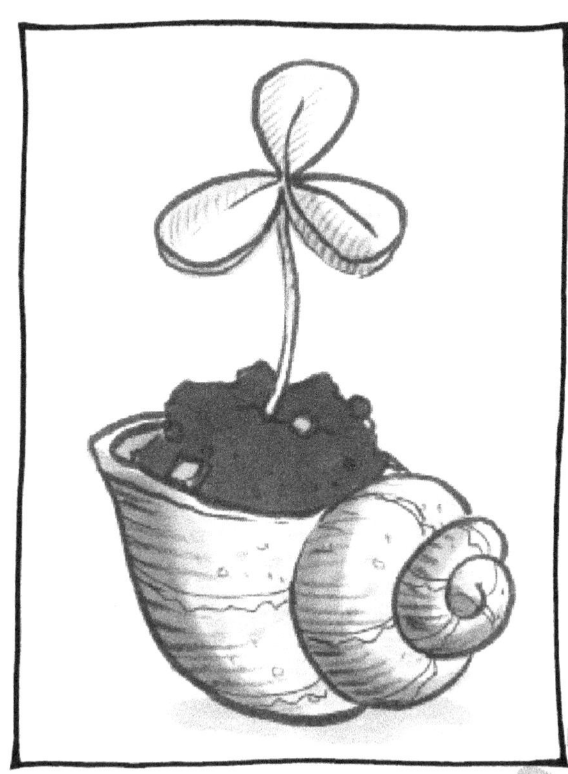

Materials: Free time, envelopes for holding seeds, something to dig with

Directions:
Tip: Some seasons will be better for this project than others.

❧ You will go on two scavenger hunts. The first involves hunting for small pots. See if you can find natural objects that can act as pots. Possibilities might include vacant snail shells, walnut shells, seashells that are washed well to remove salt, hollow pieces of wood, bamboo sections, or rocks with holes in them. You could also use recycled materials like painted yogurt containers or old, hollow plastic toys.

❧ The next hunt is for seeds. This will involve looking very closely at the wild plants growing around you. First, look to see if the plants have flowers. If they do, the seeds will follow the flowers soon. Plants have all kinds of ingenious ways of releasing seeds. Some seeds, like dandelions, fly on the breeze with little parachutes. Other seeds are catapulted, dropped, and even shot away by the plant.

❧ Find seeds that are nice and dry and place them in an envelope with the name of the plant. Germinate your seeds by putting them on a moist paper towel in a plastic bag. Tape them in a sunny window. Depending upon the seeds, it will take a couple of days for them to sprout.

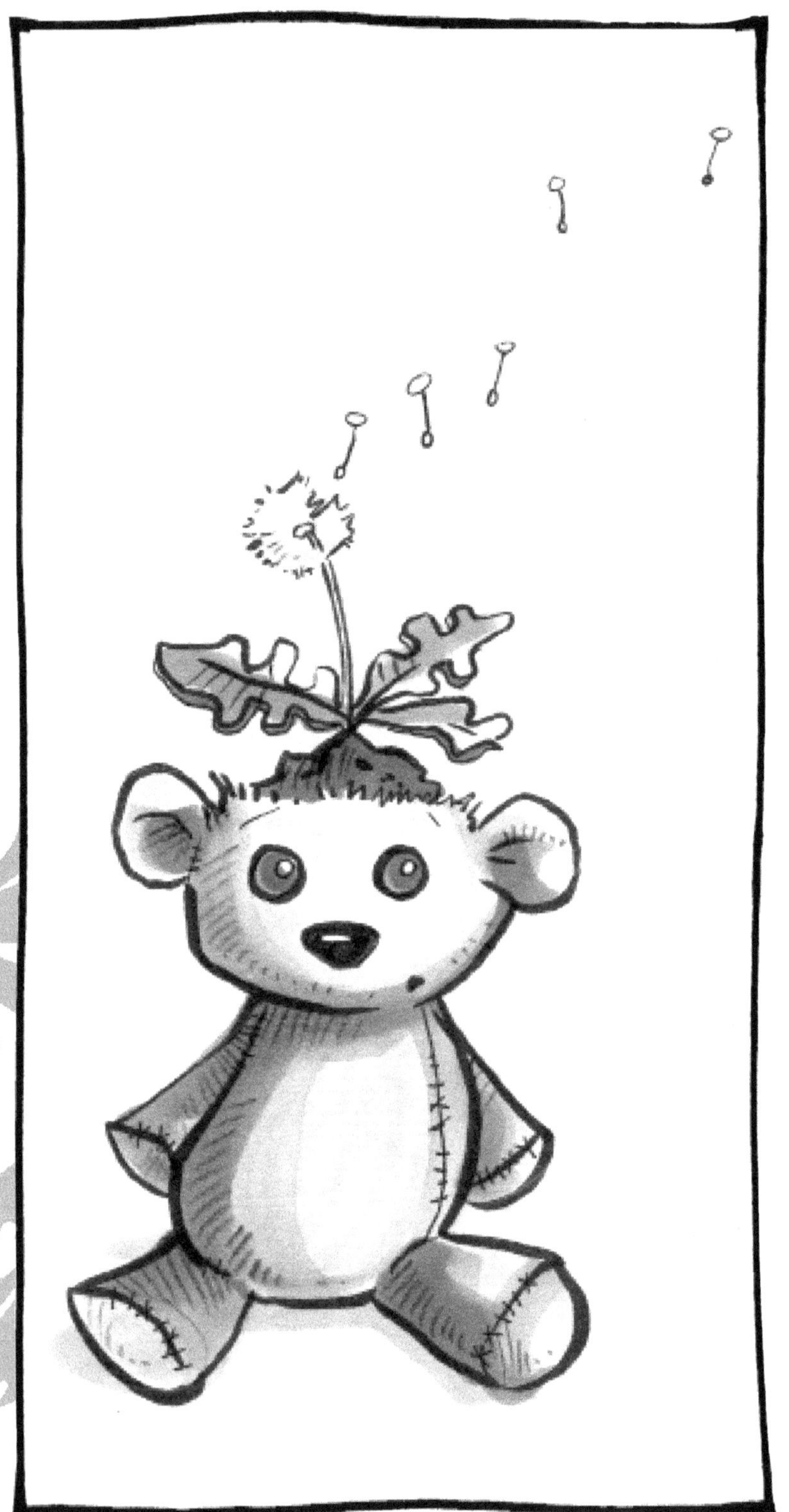

❧ Find some rich soil to fill your pots with. To do this, dig gently down through the layer of mulch under a tree until you hit soft, fluffy soil.

❧ Plant your sprouted seeds, being careful not to touch them too much. Weed seeds should not be planted very deep in the soil. Plant them in pots that are the right sizes for the plants that will grow from the seeds. Water them well, and put them in a sunny location.

Consider This: The nice thing about this garden is that it will grow very well. Weed seeds are hardy. Why do you think this plant does so well in your area? Why are its seeds so good at spreading?

Once they have sprouted, take some of the plants that were in natural pots and place them where others will have the pleasure of finding them. Imagine a hiker's surprise when they discover a weed growing from a snail shell sitting up high in an oak tree. Give some of them as gifts to friends. Nothing says, "I love you" like a dandelion planted in a seashell.

Going Further: Go to the library and find a book on wild edible and medicinal plants from your area. See if you can identify some of the weeds growing in your area. *Never* eat a wild plant unless you are with an expert who is certain that it is not poisonous. Many edible plants and poisonous plants look very similar. How do you think early people knew which plants you could eat and which ones would kill you?

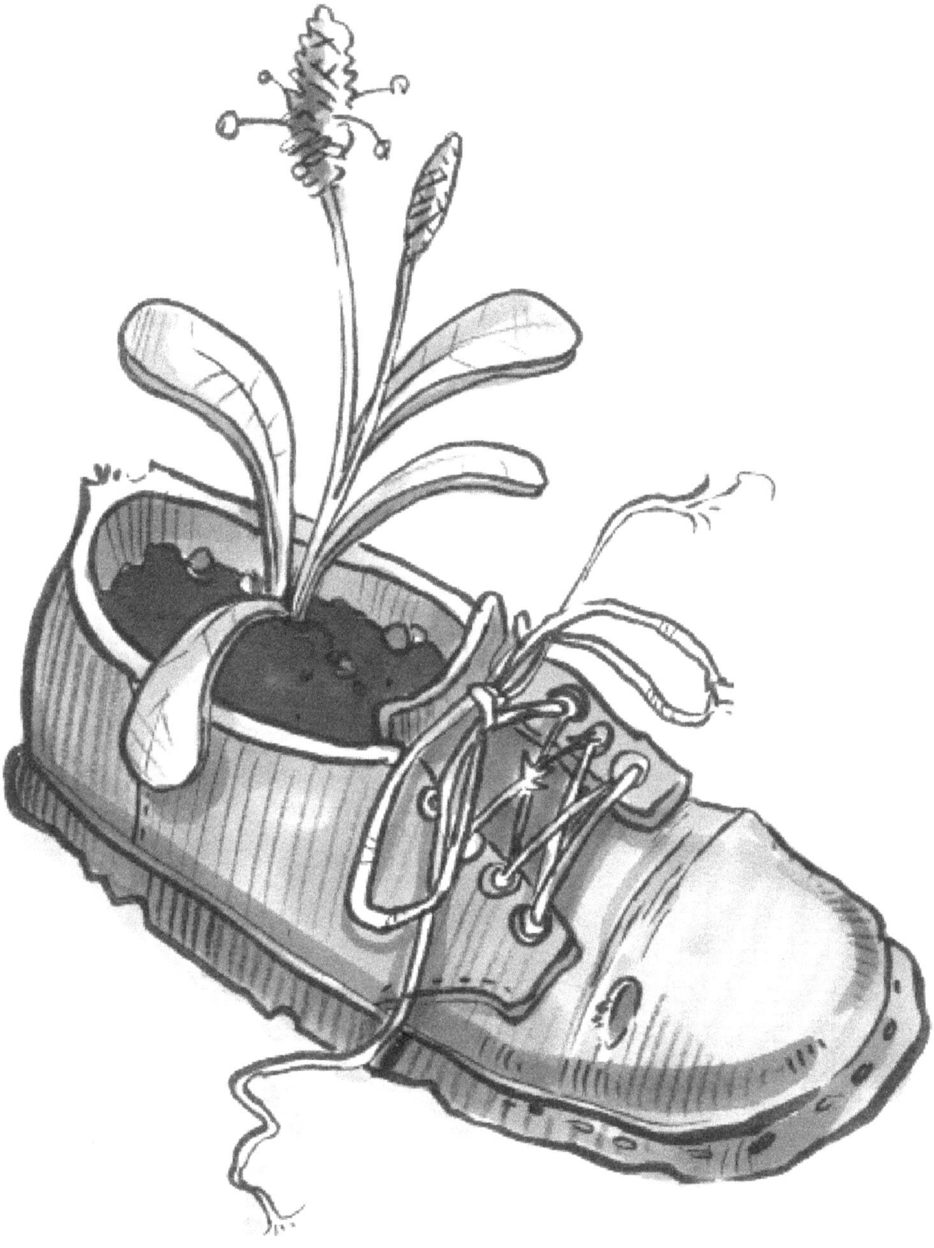

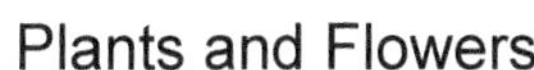

Pop-Up Drawings

Background: There are many ways to make things look three-dimensional in a drawing. We can make objects bigger to show that they are closer to us. We can overlap objects that are further back. As things get further from us, they get fainter and more grey. Look at distant mountains and see what happens to the colors of rocks and trees as they get further away. For this project, we can use all of these tricks, but we are also going to make a drawing that truly is three-dimensional using pop-ups.

Materials: Several sheets of heavy paper or card stock, scissors, glue, pieces of cardboard or cork for spacers, and drawing materials, especially colored pencils or pens

Directions:

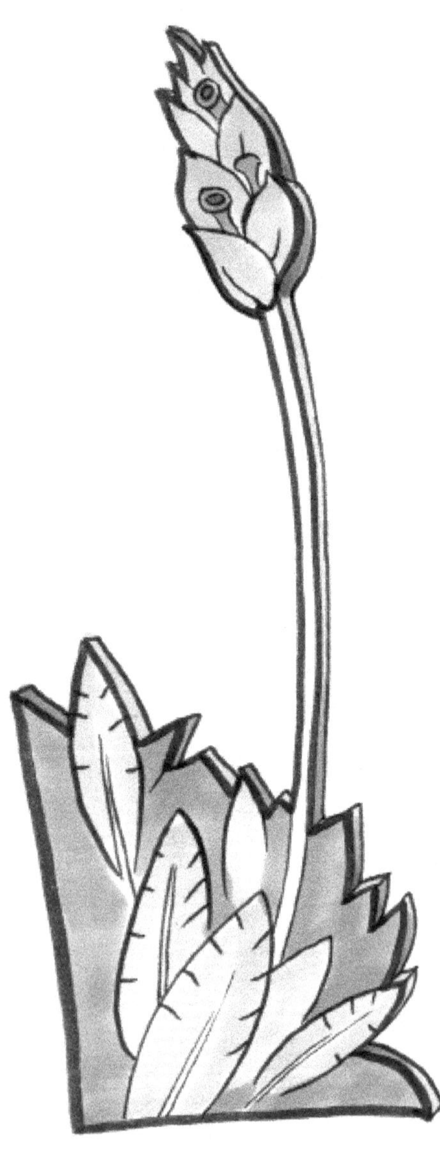

- Go to an outdoor space with a nice view and find a comfortable, shady spot to sit. Consider using a backpack to carry a snack, some water and a towel to sit on along with your art materials.

- On one of your sheets of heavy paper, you will draw the background. Draw the sky and most distant objects you can see. Start at the top and work down. Notice that as you move down the page, things get closer and closer to you. Set this sheet aside when you have finished.

- On the next sheet, draw only the middle ground. This is the area that is between the things that are close to you and the distant things you just drew. Try to use as much detail as possible. Put this sheet aside as well when it is completed.

- On the next sheet, you will draw the foreground. You will want to get really close to something nearby. Lie on your stomach and draw every detail you can see.

- Leave the background picture whole. Use scissors to cut out the empty spaces on the middle ground and foreground drawings. Leave enough paper along the edges so that the sheets won't fall apart.

- Using glue and spacers, you will create a three-dimensional scene. Attach the drawings together so that each one sticks out from the one behind it. Hang your pop-up image at eye level. If you want, you can build a shadow box out of cardboard for your drawing. You could also add more objects to your drawing, and suspend these over it with spacers as well. Consider drawing some birds sticking out above floating clouds.

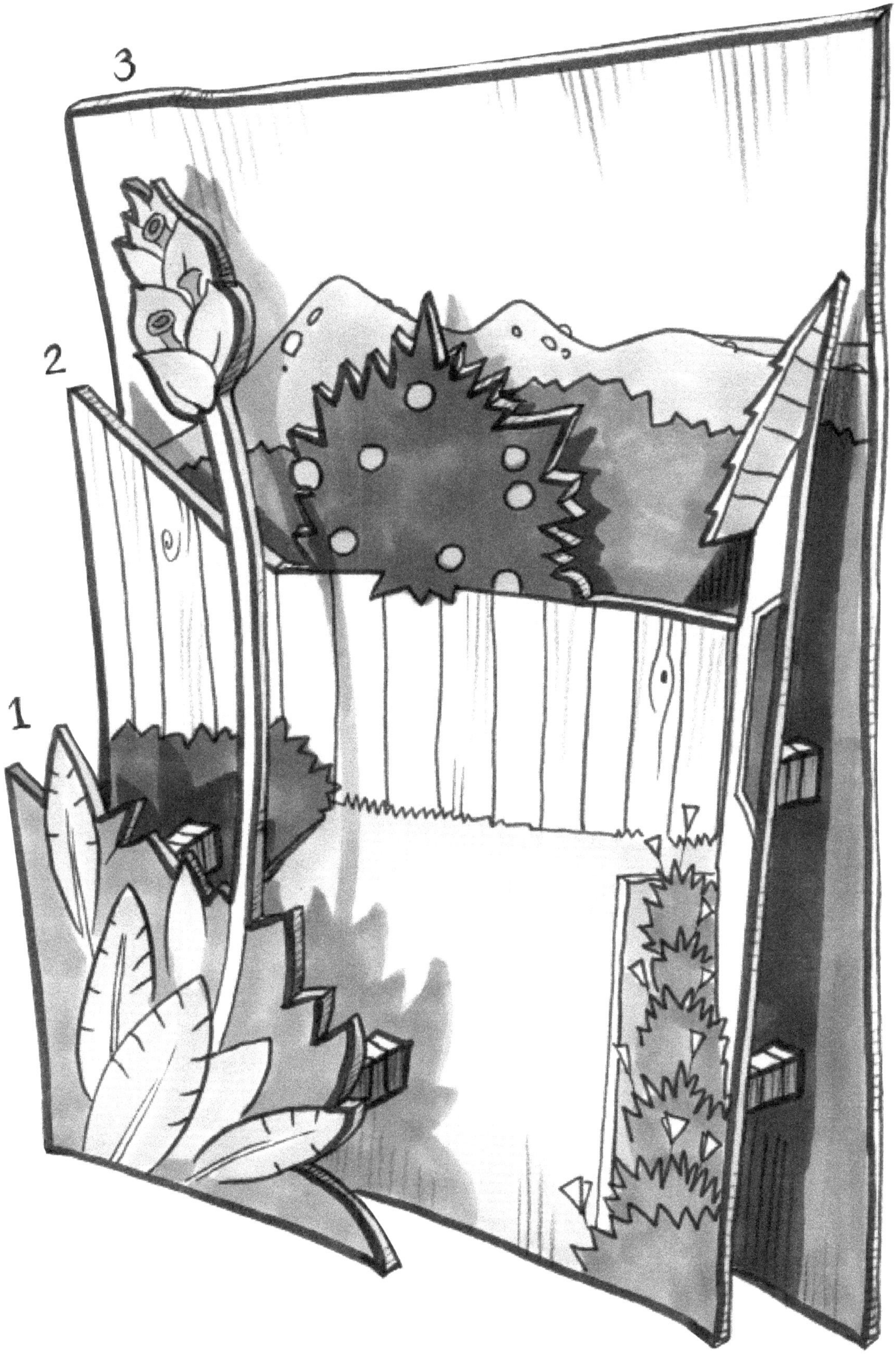

Time and Change

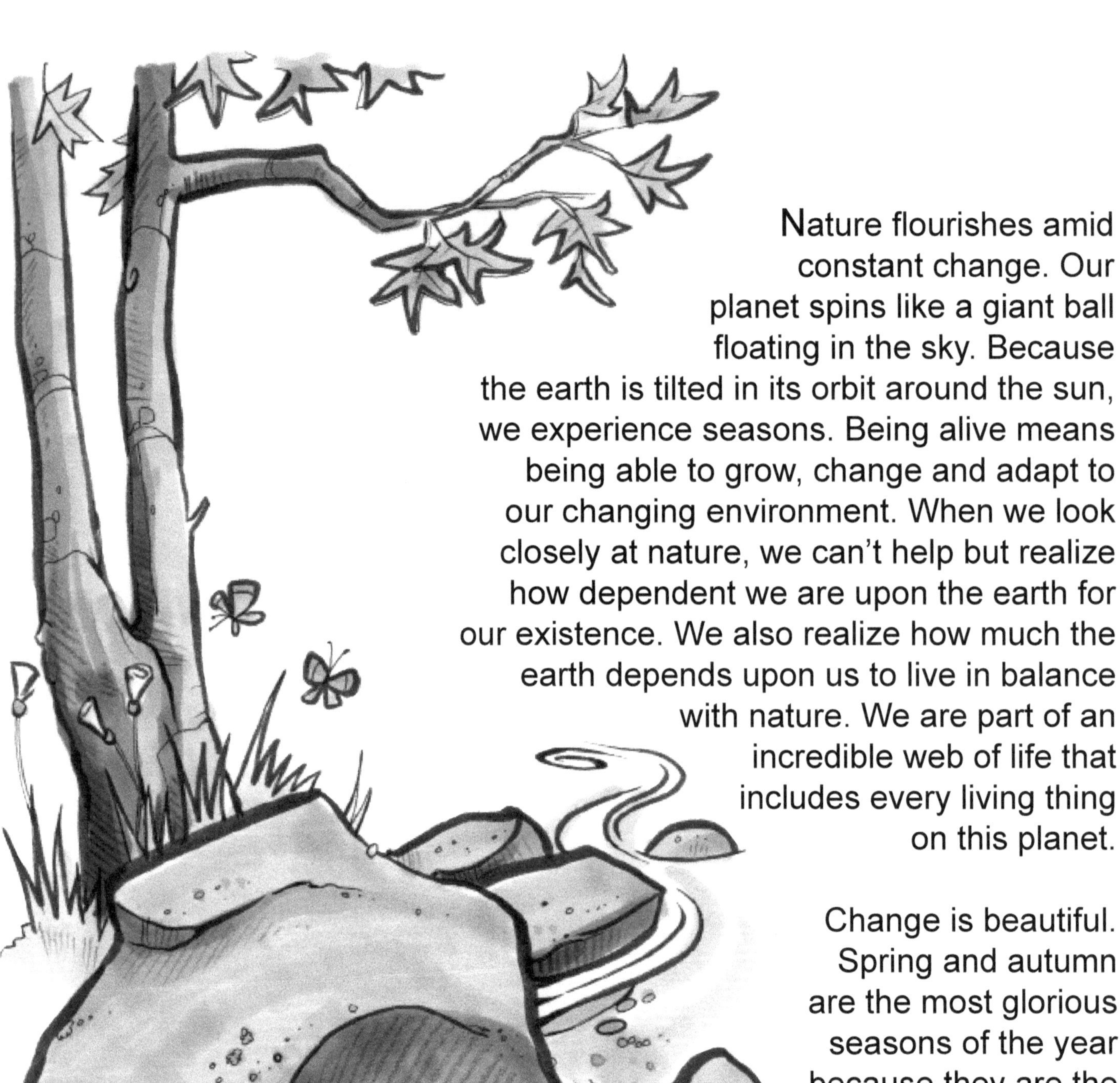

Nature flourishes amid constant change. Our planet spins like a giant ball floating in the sky. Because the earth is tilted in its orbit around the sun, we experience seasons. Being alive means being able to grow, change and adapt to our changing environment. When we look closely at nature, we can't help but realize how dependent we are upon the earth for our existence. We also realize how much the earth depends upon us to live in balance with nature. We are part of an incredible web of life that includes every living thing on this planet.

Change is beautiful. Spring and autumn are the most glorious seasons of the year because they are the transition times. In these seasons of change, nature is preparing for longer

4

days in summer
or shorter winter days. Think of the
changes that happen in spring and
autumn where you live.

As artists, we often want to try to illustrate and
share these beautiful, miraculous changes
our world goes through. But we find ourselves
challenged with how to show time and change in
a drawing. After all, when we draw a landscape,
it is frozen in time on our paper as the real scene
before us changes every moment of every day.

In this chapter, we will explore some creative ways
that artists can make art that shows movement,
growth and change. This would also be a good
time to reflect upon the changes
people have brought to
wild landscapes and
to direct some of our
creativity into thinking
of ways that we
can live in peace
and harmony on the
earth as time continues to
pass.

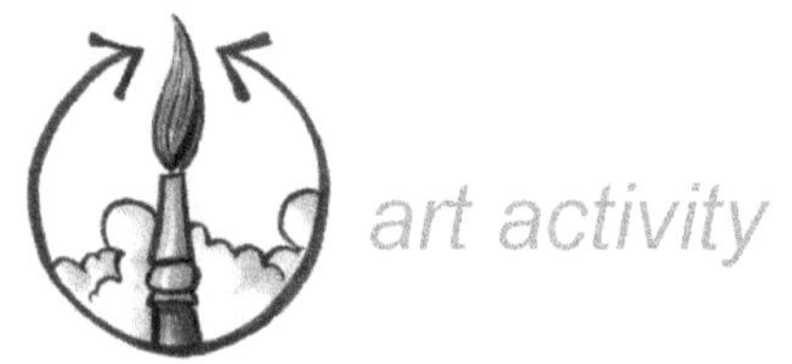

Leaf Exposures

Background: Plants can turn sunlight into energy. When you look at fresh green leaves on a tree, the green color you are seeing comes from chlorophyll. Chlorophyll is responsible for photosynthesis, which helps plants turn sunlight into sugars. Almost all life on earth exists because of chlorophyll. If we block the sunlight from reaching part of a leaf, the healthy green color of the chlorophyll is lost. We are going to use this fact to create sun prints on leaves.

In this project, you will learn a primitive type of photography. Photography is the art of making images using light.

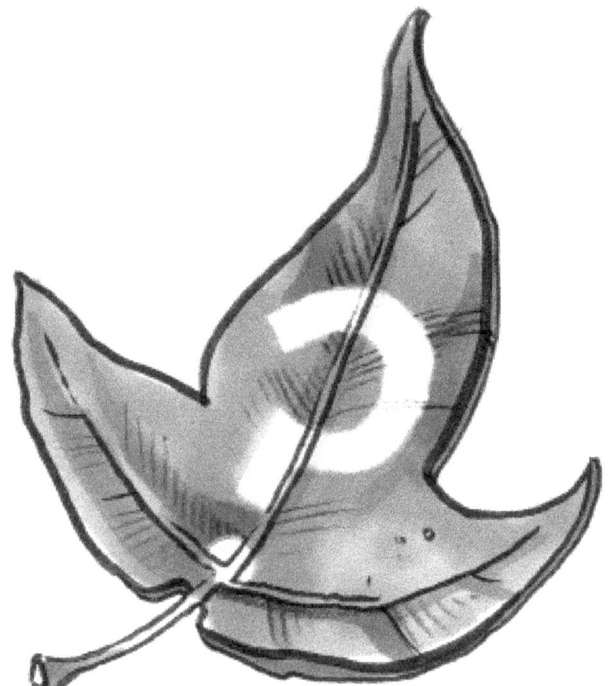

Materials: Card stock or thin cardboard, scissors, pencil, paperclips

Directions:

- Think about what type of image you would like to be able to see on a leaf. Would you make a drawing or a design? Draw your ideas below.

- Draw your final design on card stock. Think about the size of the leaves you may attach it to.

- Carefully cut out your design with scissors to create a small stencil.

- You are going to paperclip your stencil to a leaf that is still attached to a tree. It is helpful to go to the sunniest side of the tree to hunt for your leaf. Try several different types of trees to see which leaves will work best for your stencil. Make sure that your stencil will cover only part of the leaf. When you find the perfect leaf, attach your stencil with the paperclip.

- After a few days have passed, check on your leaf. Carefully lift the stencil to see if it has made an image yet.

- When the image is clear, take a picture of it while it is still on the tree. Then, pick your leaf and give it to a friend.

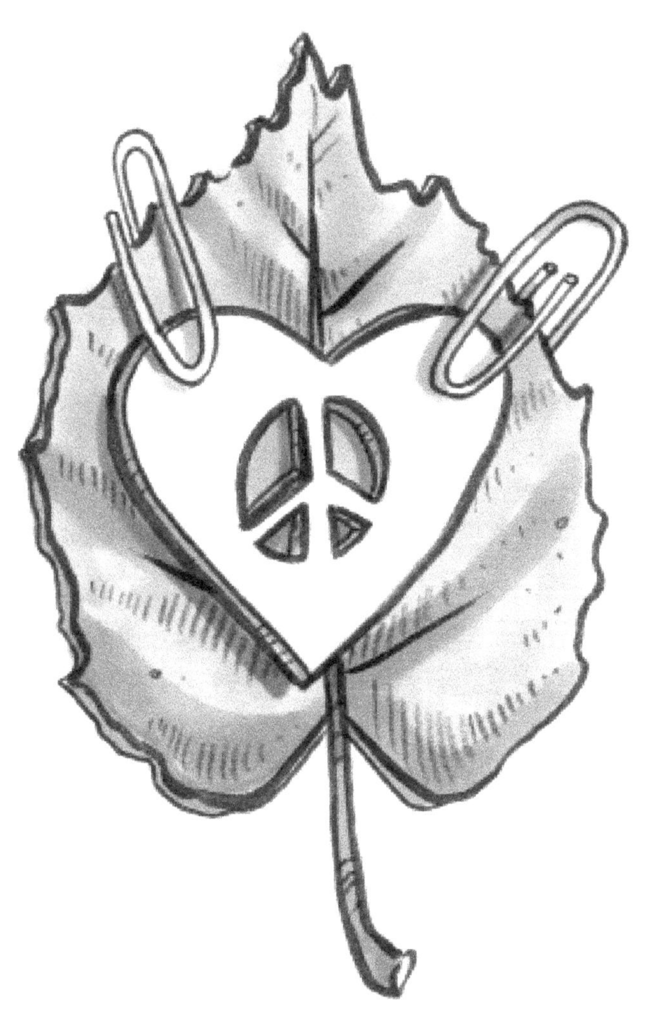

Going Further: How could you get even more details in your design? Some photographers have attached actual film negatives to a leaf and exposed realistic images in chlorophyll. How could you use leaf prints to help people recognize the beauty of the trees around them? Try making leaf prints of all the letters in your name, and pin the leaves up in your room.

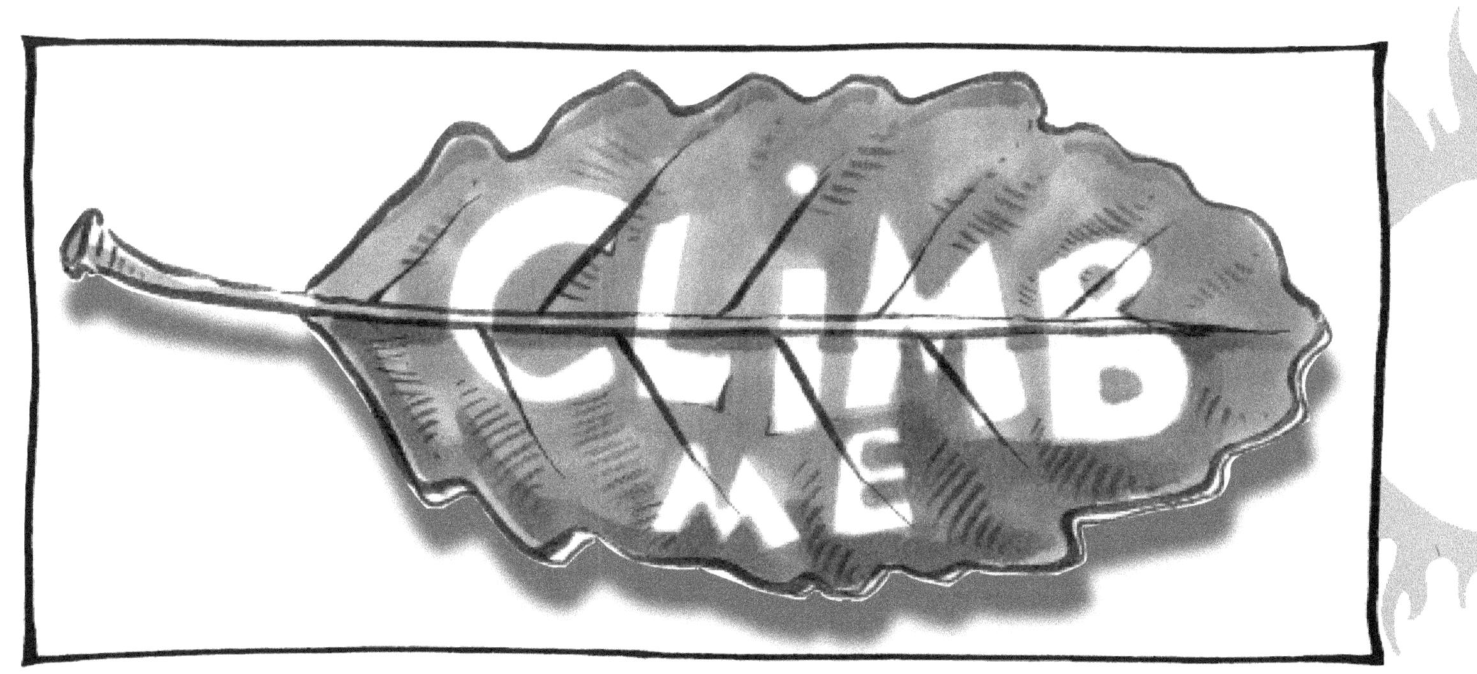

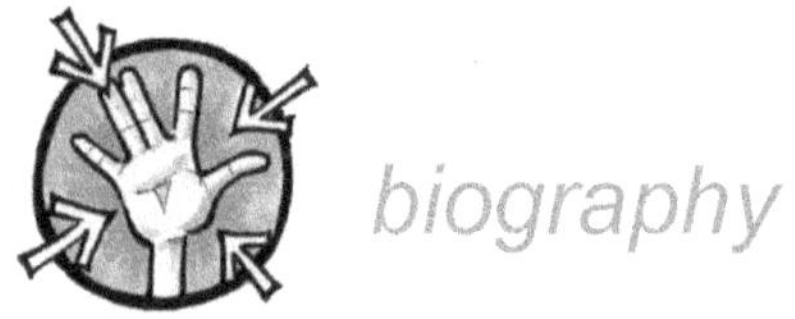

Focus on Kim Abeles

California artist Kim Abeles has come up with a unique technique for creating stenciled artworks. The artist noticed how the smog in Los Angeles would coat the windows of her car with a film of soot. This gave her the idea to create smog prints.

Kim Abeles cuts out elaborate stencils and sticks them to sheets of glass. She then places these on the roof of her apartment building in the city and waits for the smog to settle on them. When the stencils are removed, the clean glass is a contrast to the smogged glass and a ghost-like image is visible. It is art made from pollution! She seals them and puts them on display.

Her images are often of famous early American paintings. This was a time when artists made paintings about the beauty of progress and development. Abeles says she is trying to show that we are a land still influenced by nineteenth century thought. She has printed dollar bills in smog. She did a series of smogged plates with the faces of U.S. presidents and quotes from comments they made about the environment. Since air quality is something that is sometimes difficult for us to see, Kim Abeles has found a beautiful way of making it visible and raising people's awareness of the environment.

Why do you think Kim Abeles does portraits of U.S. presidents on her plates? What do they have to do with pollution?

____
____

How is the air quality where you live? How about the water quality?

____
____

What are some environmental problems where you live?

____
____

How can artists help to solve these problems?

____
____

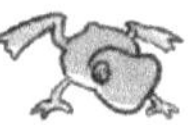

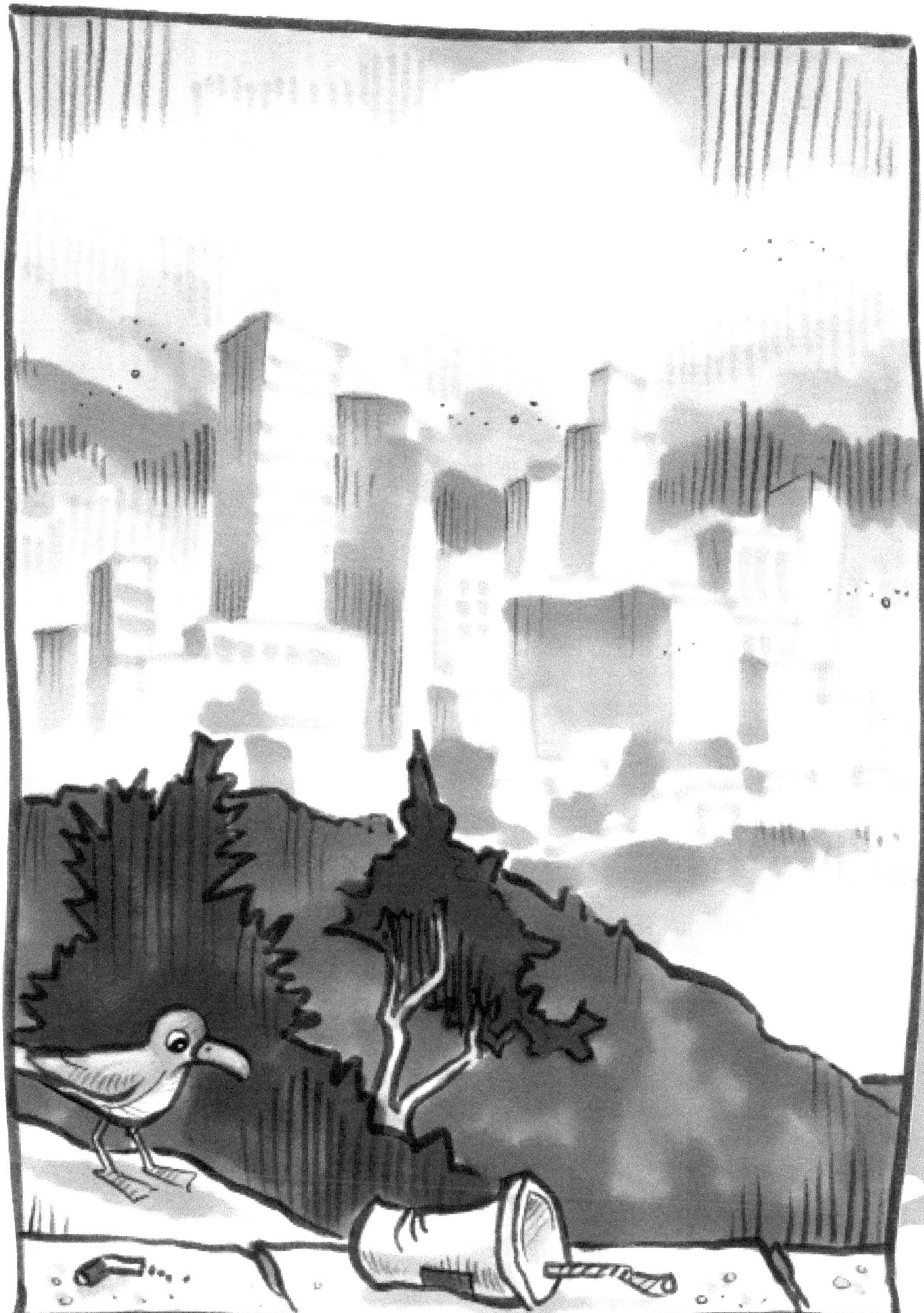

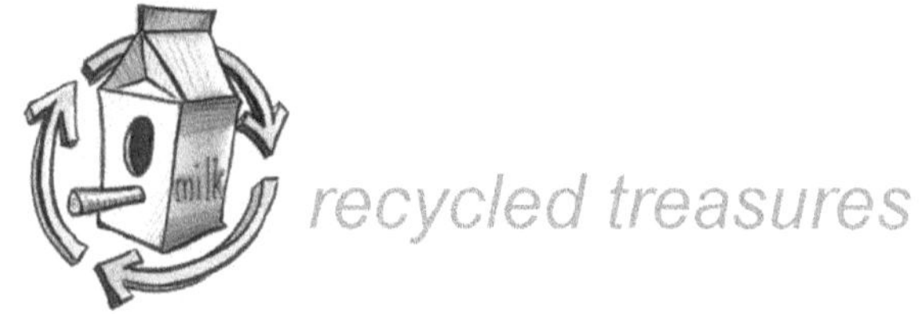

recycled treasures

The Six Directions

Background: Few people have ever lived as in harmony with the natural world as the Native Americans. Native peoples tended the wild landscape as though it was a garden and realized on the deepest level that whatever happens to the earth, happens to us as well.

Many Native American tribes have variations on the concept of the six directions.   The six directions are the four cardinal directions of north, south, east and west, plus up and down. Each of these directions has colors and symbols related to them that vary according to traditions and regions. They are used to tell stories that talk about stages of life, the four seasons, and times of the day. Below you will find a basic chart of some of these symbols. The Native American medicine wheel ceremony is about finding balance between these directions.

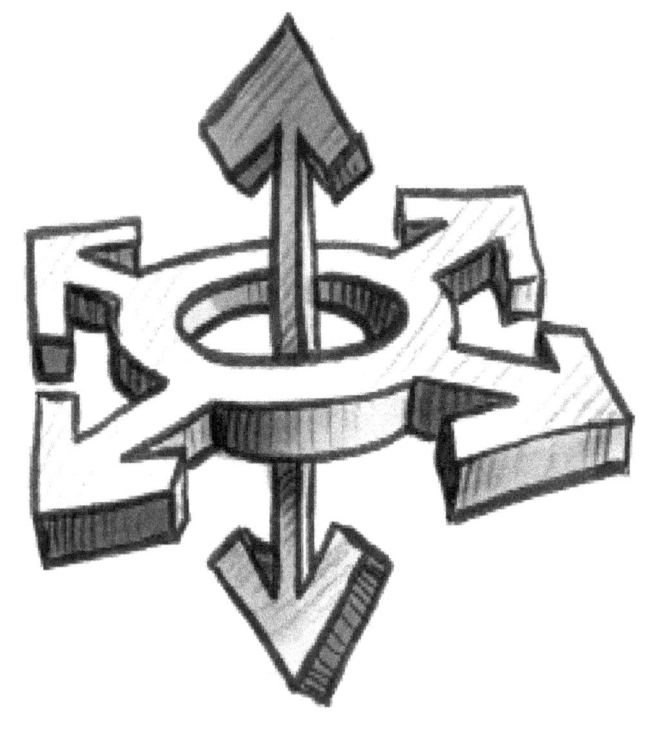

Direction	Color	Symbolism
East	Yellow	childhood, springtime, sunrise, sprouting
South	Red	youth maturing, growth, summer, mid-day
West	Black	middle age, autumn, dusk, going to seed
North	White	old age, wisdom, winter, evening, dying back
Down	Green	mother earth, the body
Up	Blue	father sky, the spirit

Why do you think these particular colors were chosen for each of these directions? *For example:* What would "white" have to do with winter, the north, and old age?

____

____

____

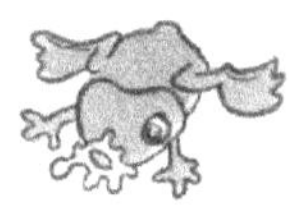

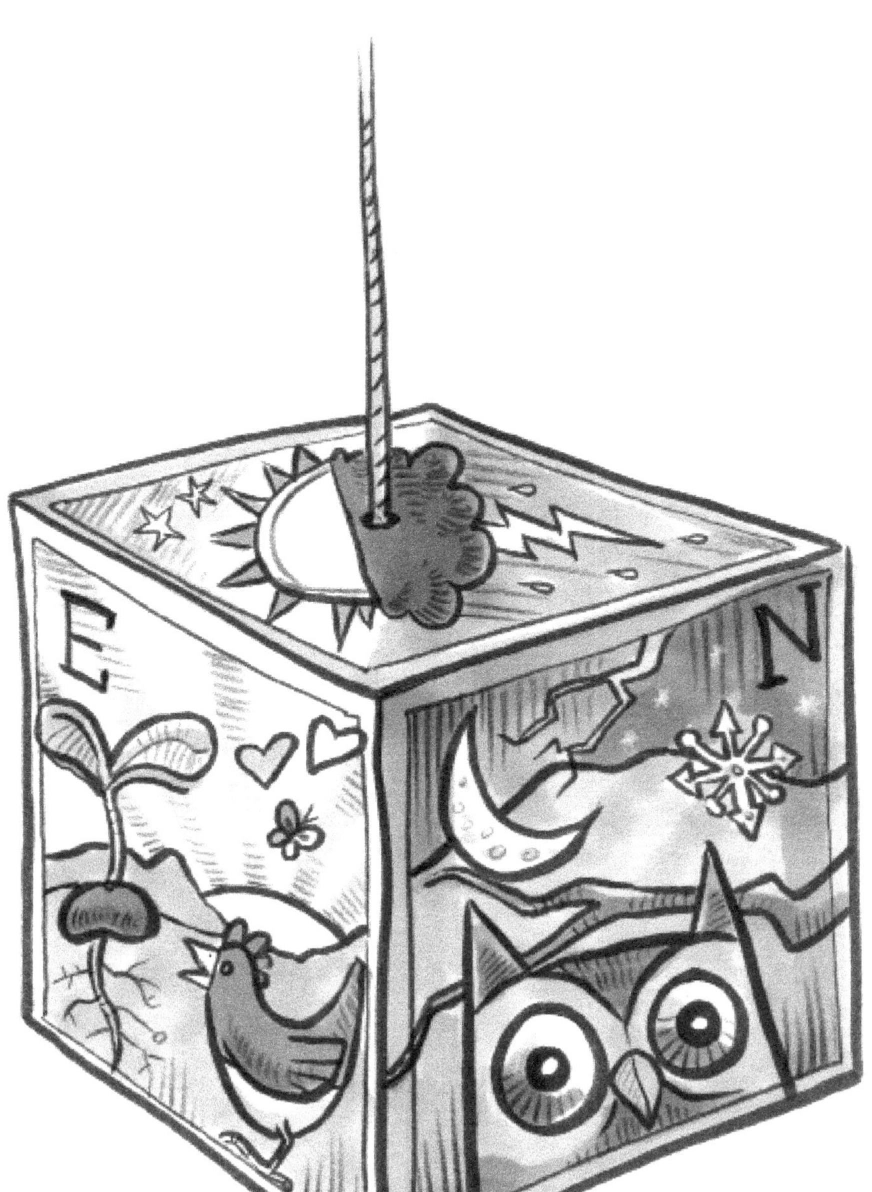

Materials: 6 pieces of cardboard cut into squares, glue or tape, drawing and coloring materials (thick paint would be great), other art materials and collage materials that may appeal to you

Directions:

❧ Make a wish for the future. Put a lot of thought into something that you would like to have happen. Try to create a wish that is not for yourself alone, but for the entire planet. Write it down on a small sheet of paper, and don't tell it to anyone.

❧ Take the six pieces of cardboard and assemble them to form a cube. The best way to do this is to put tape on the inside to hold the pieces together, then to neatly tape over the edges.

❧ As you are taping the cube together, seal your wish inside of it. You could also throw in a few beans or seeds so your box will rattle, reminding you of your wish.

❧ You are going to design each side of your cube to represent one of the six directions. Before you begin, read about each side's symbols in the chart. Think about what these symbols mean to you and the thoughts, pictures or designs that come to your mind. You can draw and write. Have fun!

❧ As you draw, make sure that you put the sides in the right position. Up should be opposite of down. East is opposite of west. North is opposite of south.

❧ When you display your completed artwork, you may want to hang it by a string. Try to orient it with the true directions. To find north, simply put a stick in the ground straight up and down at noon. If you are in the northern hemisphere, its shadow is pointing north.

❧ You can hang your finished design by attaching a string to the "up" side. Like a compass, you can spin it so it points in the four directions now.

Questions: Look at the opposite sides on your cube. Do those sides seem to be very different from each other?

____

____

____

How are your east designs different from your west designs? How about your north and south? Up and down?

____

____

____

Going Further: Using the Internet or books from the library, research more about the medicine wheel ceremony. Think about the pyramids that can be found in Central America and in Egypt. These also are split into four directions that line up with the directions of north, south, east and west. Why do you think cultures from all around the world have found it so important to understand these directions? What do they tell us about the sun and seasons?

____

____

____

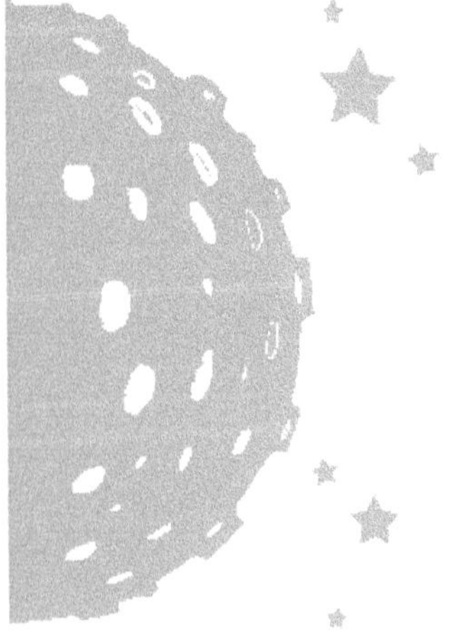

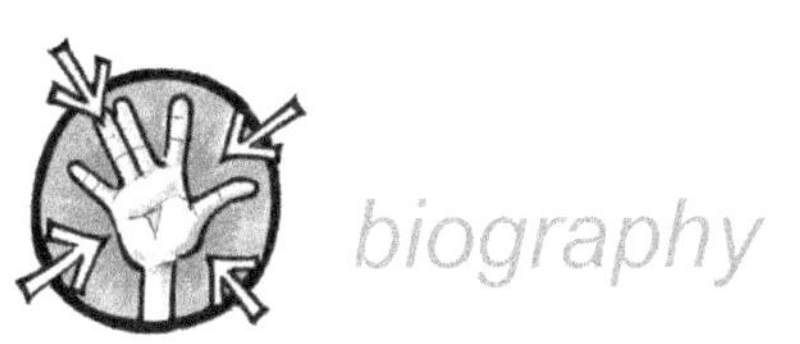

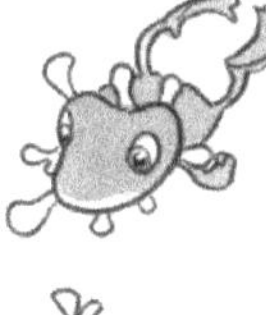

Focus on Tibetan Sand Paintings

For centuries, monks in Tibet have created an art form known as sand painting. Sand paintings are created in a geometric shape called a mandala. Mandala means "circle" in Sanskrit. There are many variations on mandalas. They are usually created with traditional geometric patterns and sacred symbols. The mandala is meant to be a symbol for the entire world.

It takes several days of very patient work to construct a sand painting. Colored sand is slowly applied to the painting one grain at a time as it flows through a small metal funnel called a chak-pur. The chak-pur is raked with a special stick, and friction makes the colored sand flow from the tip like sand runs through an hourglass.

The vibrant, colorful, intricate design slowly grows as the monks meditate and wish good thoughts upon all of the earth's inhabitants. Then, at the end of the ceremony, they bring out a broom and sweep the mandala away.

It seems unusual that somebody would work so hard on something only to destroy it. For the monks, however, the sand painting is just a metaphor for the beautiful impermanence of life and nature. Part of what makes a flower so special is the fact that it is only there for a short period of time. The monks enjoy the painting as it is being created, and then sweep it away so that they can go on with their lives uncluttered.

It is interesting to know that the Navajo Indians also have an ancient tradition of sand painting. They developed it without ever talking to the Tibetans, but their tradition has some similarities.

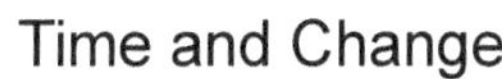

Like the Tibetan monks, they create designs made out of colored sand that point in four directions. They are created by the medicine man in the tribe to help heal people, and like the Tibetan mandalas, they are swept away after they are created.

Exploration: Make a work of art that is temporary. Put a lot of time and care into making something outdoors. It could be a sand castle or a design out of rocks or anything. After it is done, take it apart so there is no sign that it ever existed.

Questions: What did you end up making? (Sketch your artwork or attach a photo in the space below.)

____

____

____

Did a part of you want to keep your artwork whole? How did it make you feel once you swept your work away?

____

____

____

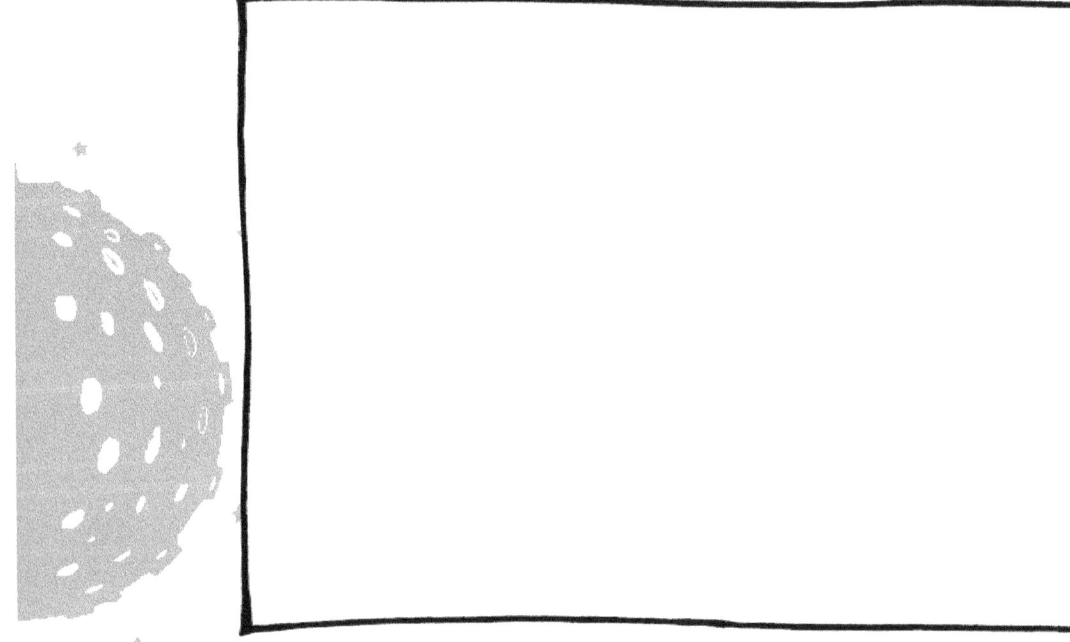

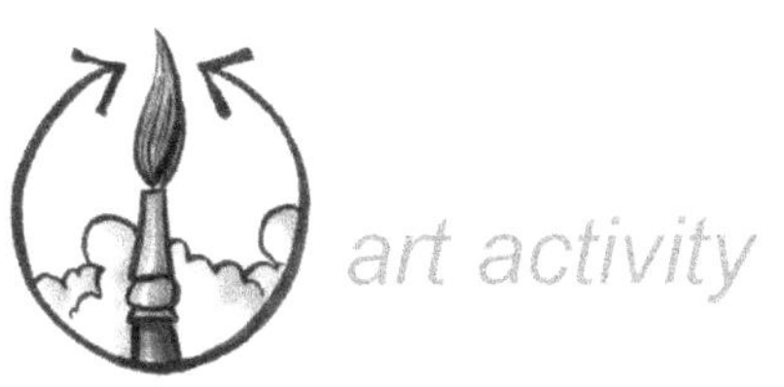

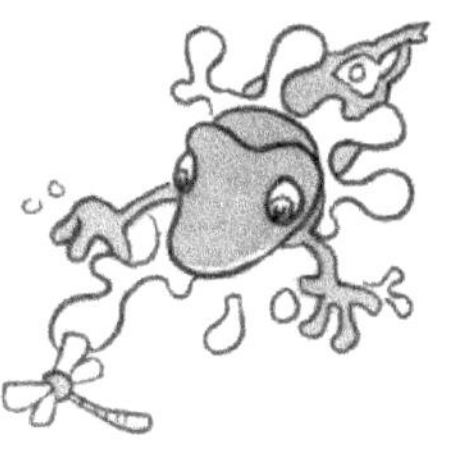

Nature Comics

Background: A drawing is frozen in time. It can't move. It can't change. If you draw a child, in a hundred years that child will be a very old person, but the drawing will still show a child. Drawings can't show time. That is, unless they are comics!

You can think of ancient Egyptian hieroglyphics as a type of comics. Hieroglyphics are a series of drawings that tell a story and show movement. Comics are like filmstrips, in a sense, where you look at each frame, and together, they illustrate change.

Nature is full of stories. Nothing sits still, and everything changes. For this project, you will go for a walk, looking closely at some of those changes. Then you will illustrate the changes as a comic.

Materials: Paper, rulers, pencil, black pen, colored pencils.

Directions:

- Go out into the world and look for something that changes and grows. You might make a comic that shows how the seasons change a plant in your garden. Your comic might show different creatures that visit your yard and eat each other as part of the food chain. Perhaps your comic will show the changes that have taken place in your neighborhood as trees were cut down to make room for houses. To find a subject for your comic, brainstorm things that change over time. Once you have your idea, make rough sketches on a piece of scratch paper to plan out what you will draw in each of the different panels. There are panels on the next pages to help you make your first comic.

- In the first panel, you will want to create a unique title for your comic. Make some fun, unusual letters for your title. Below you will find some examples:

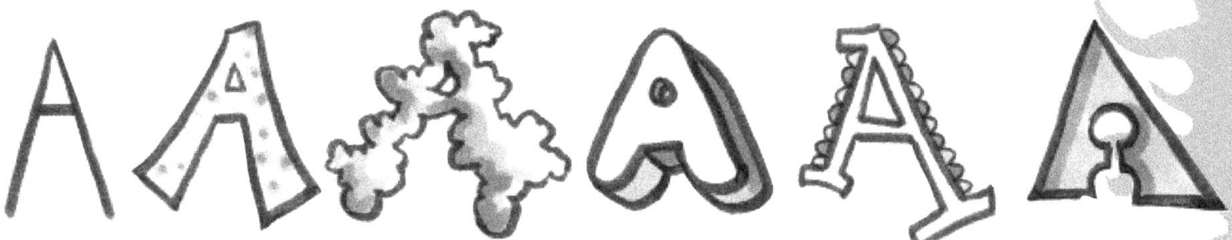

- Sketch your comic out very lightly in pencil. Think about changing the angle of your drawing from frame to frame. For example, make things close-up in some frames and far away in others. In some panels draw a bird's-eye view, and in others, draw a worm's-eye view.

This comic was inspired by the discovery that some species of wild bees sleep at night in wild flowers that close around them like sleeping bags rather than always returning to the hive. (continued on the following page)

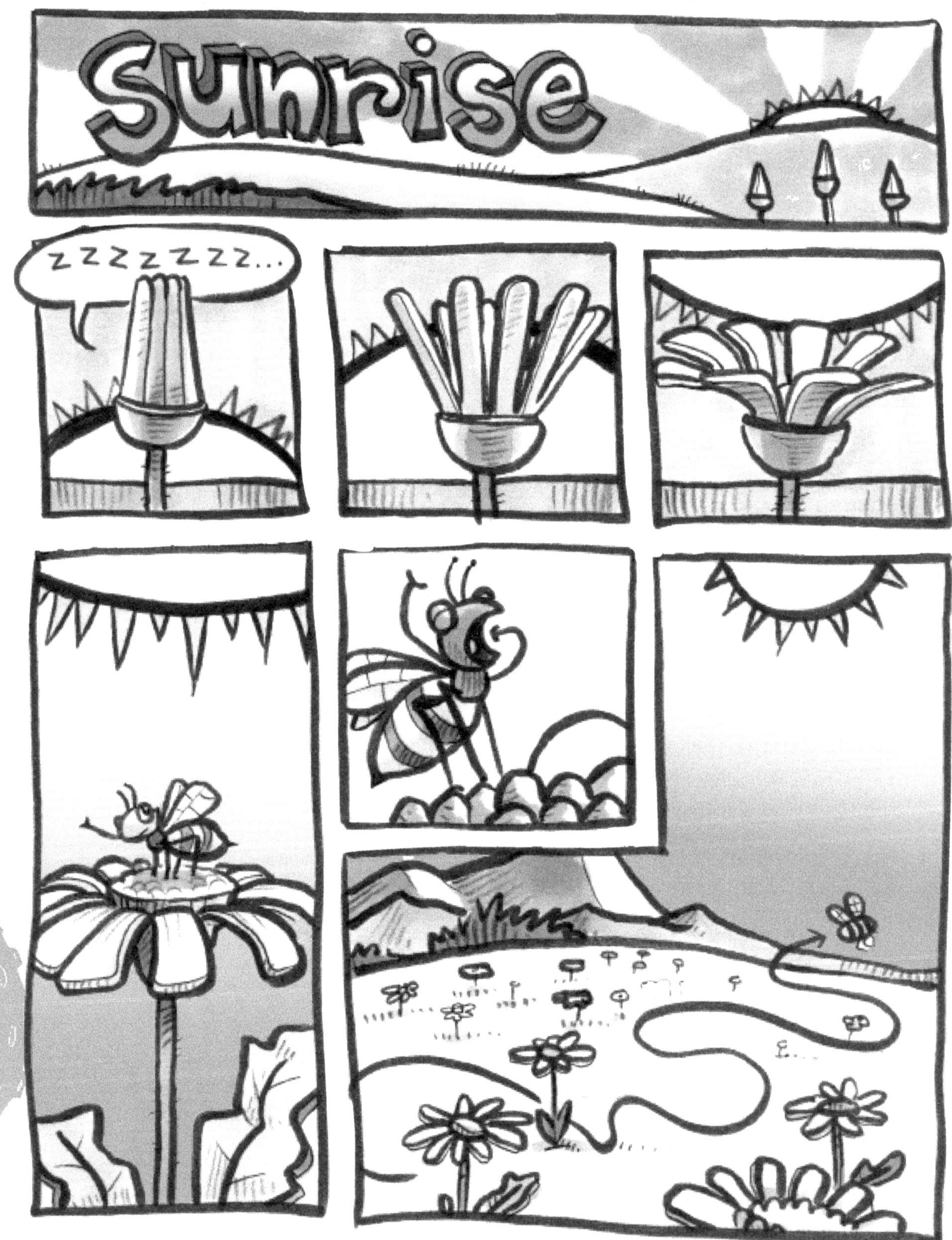

Sunrise
Zzzzzzzz...

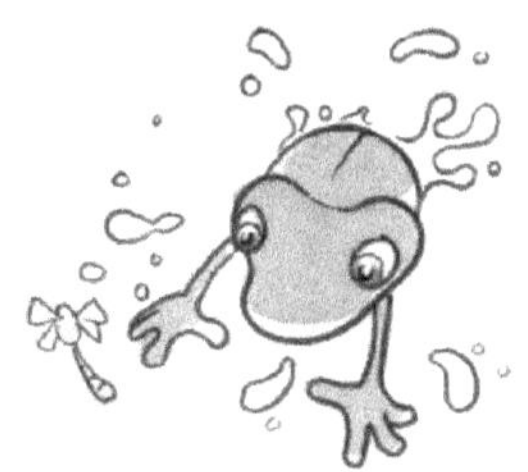

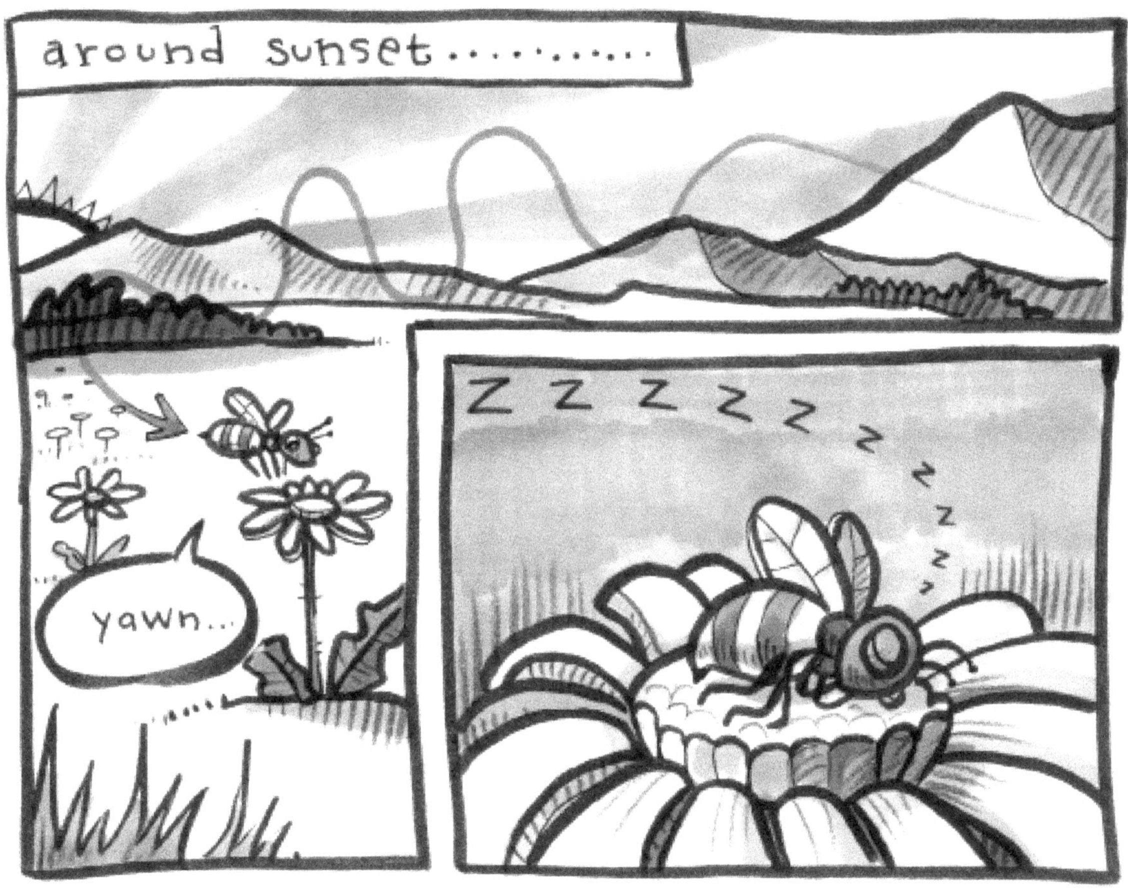

❧ Outline your drawings in pen, and erase the extra pencil lines. Then, add color or shading to your design.

❧ Share your comic with others. If you have a scanner, scan your design into the computer and e-mail it to friends and family. Or, print it out and sneak surprise copies into your neighbors' newspapers early in the morning.

Going Further: Could you make an entire comic book? Think of a theme first. If you had the opportunity to say something to thousands of people, what would it be? Would you want to make people laugh or smile? Would you want them to think about something?

____

____

____

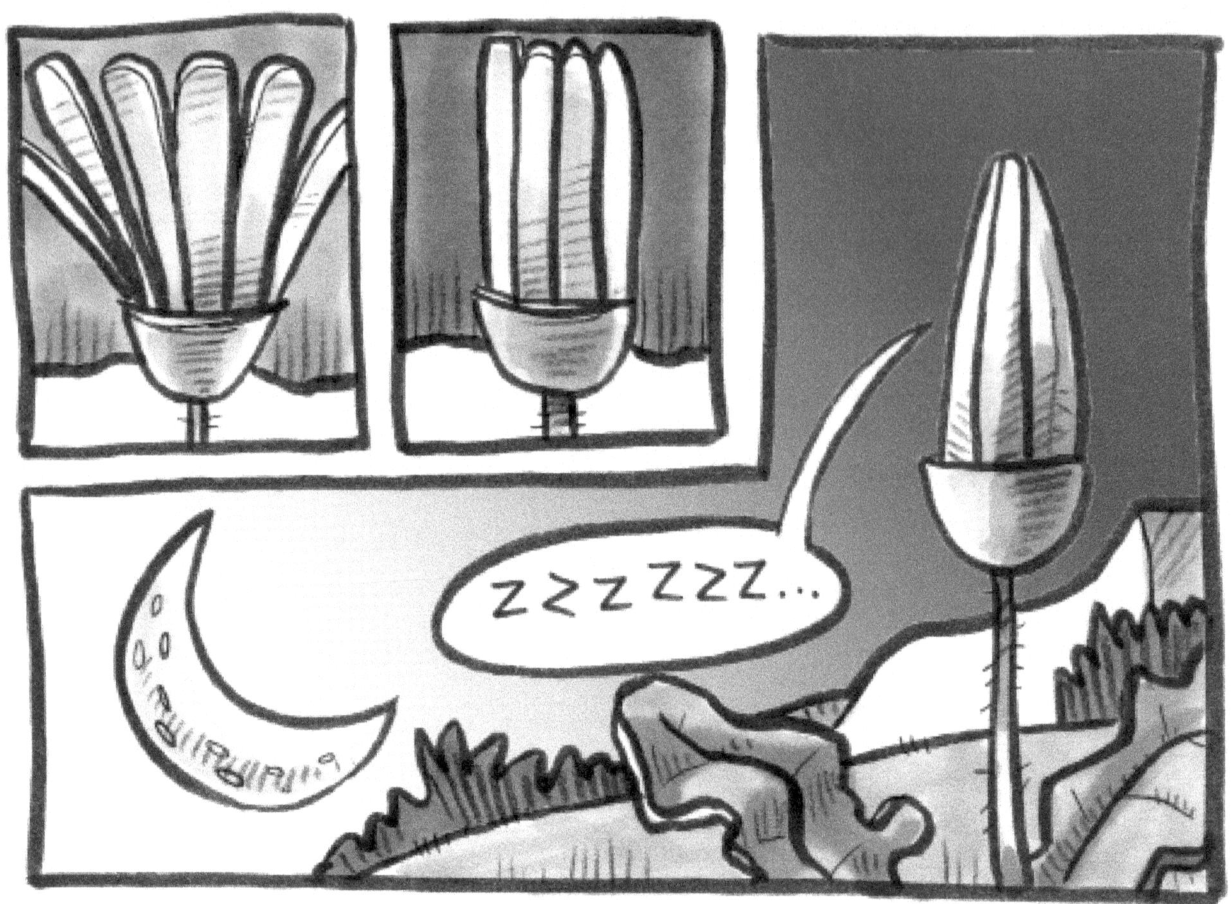

Use the space to the right to create your own nature comic.

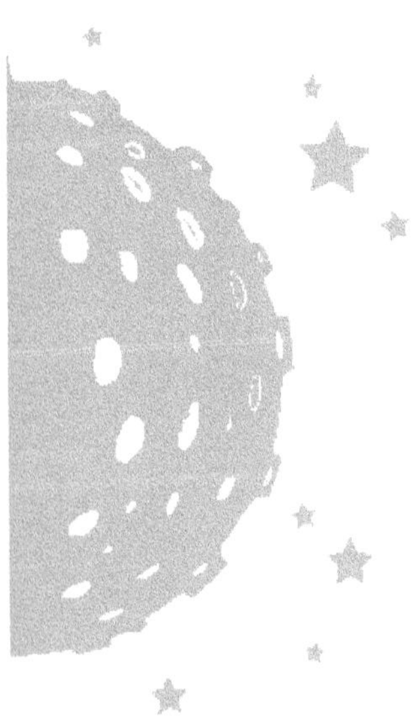

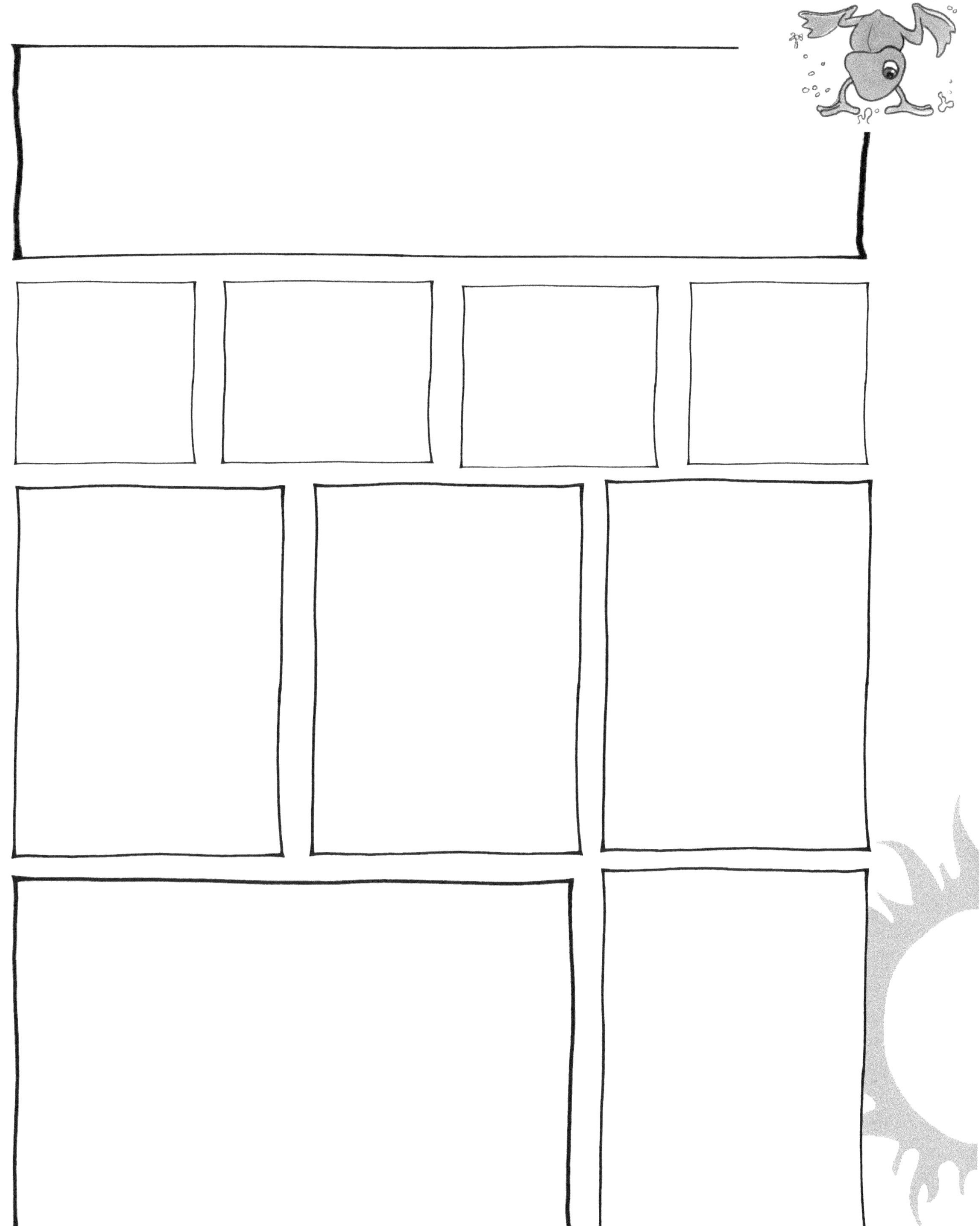

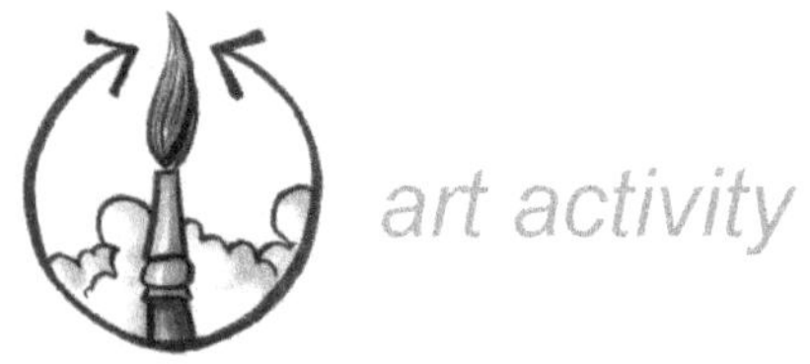

Flipbooks!

Background: Have you noticed that the drawings of frogs in the upper right-hand corner of this book are all a little different? This book contains a secret flipbook! Try holding the book as shown in the picture and slowly fanning through the pages. Amazing! We can make drawings that move. For this project, you will learn the basics of animation and make your own flipbook.

Practice: Look at the animation of the tadpole one page at a time. Notice how it changes just a little bit in each drawing. In the squares below, try completing an animation of the sun rising over a mountain.

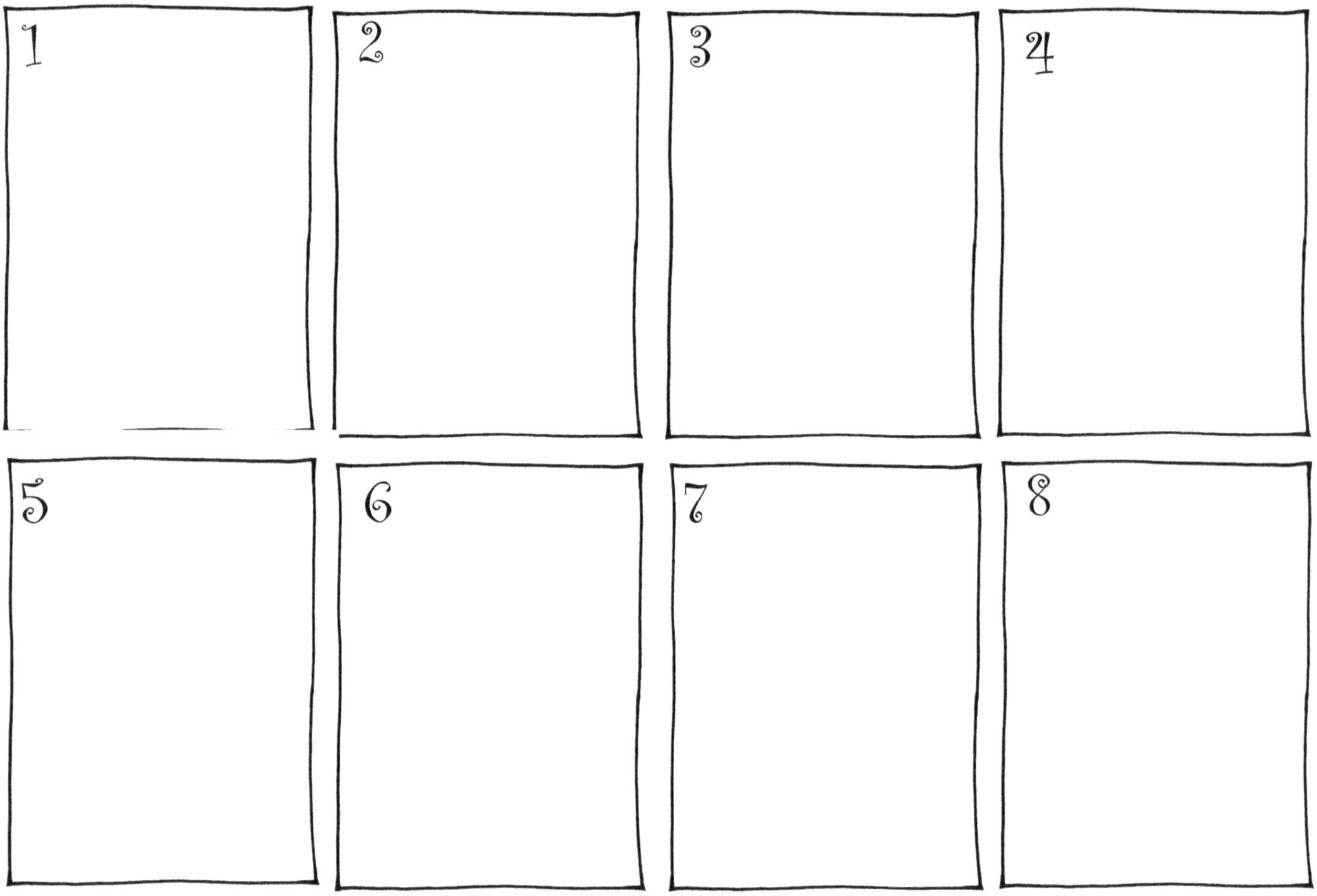

1	2	3	4
5	6	7	8

Materials: Pencil or pen, colored pencil, clear tape, blank notepads about 3"x4" or a stack of very cleanly cut paper of similar dimensions — large sticky-note pads work very well.

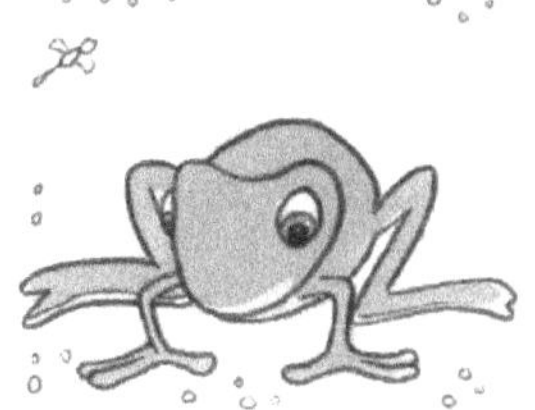

Directions:

- If you are using loose paper, make a stack of 50-100 sheets of paper and tap the stack on a table to get all the pieces lined up.

- Wrap Scotch tape tightly around the end of the book as shown in the illustration.

- Start on the back page and draw the first frame of the picture you are going to animate.

- Lay the second page over this. You should be able to see your first drawing through the paper. Make this drawing a little different to show movement.

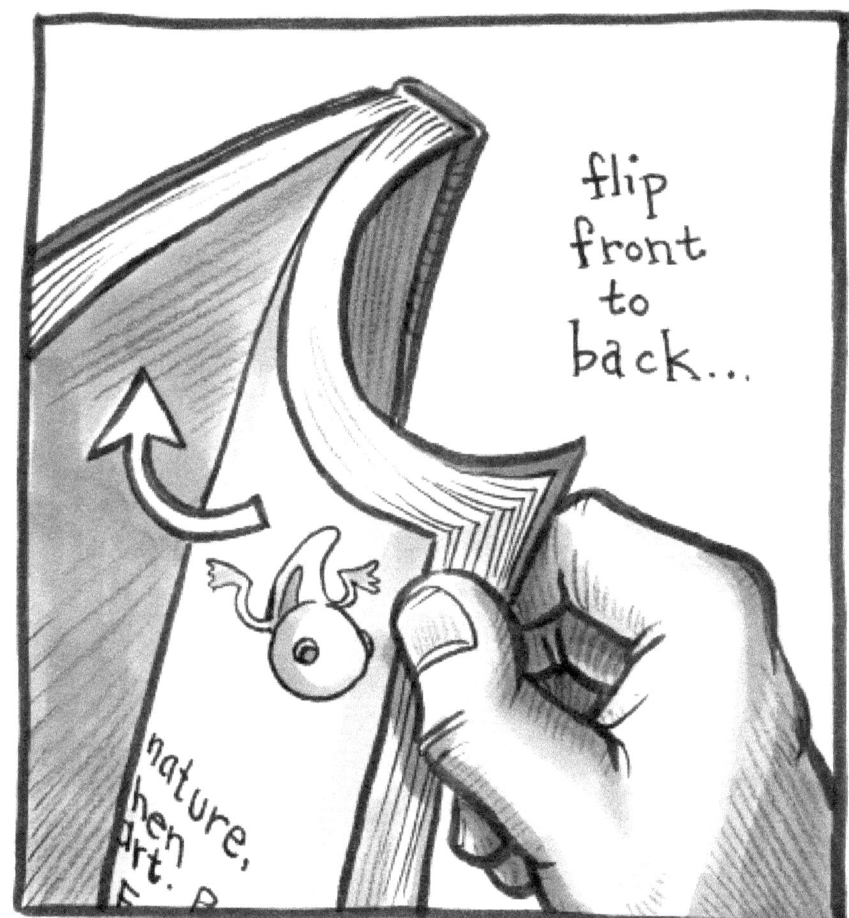

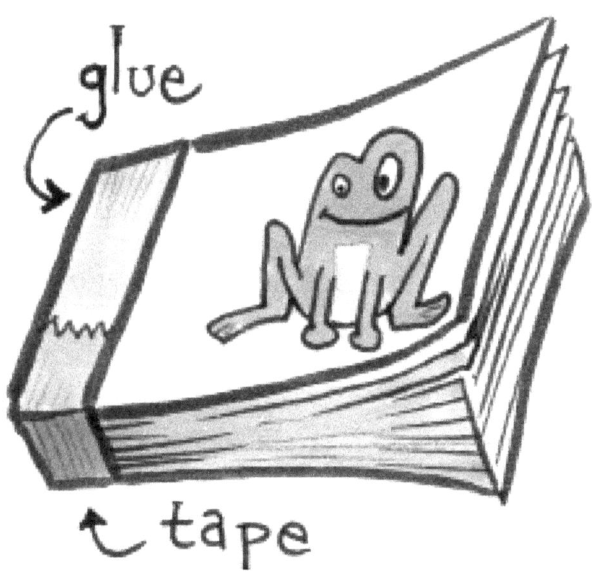

- Continue laying down pages and drawing. After you have about ten pages, you can start to check your progress by fanning the book as shown in the illustration on the next page.

- When you finish your book, you can go back and add color if you like.

- Make a cover for your flipbook out of heavier paper, and create a title for it.

Observation: The next time you watch a cartoon, think about the amount of work that went into creating all of the drawings. Look closely to see the details the artists put into all the moving parts. What are some things that animators can create that still aren't possible with cameras?

____

____

____

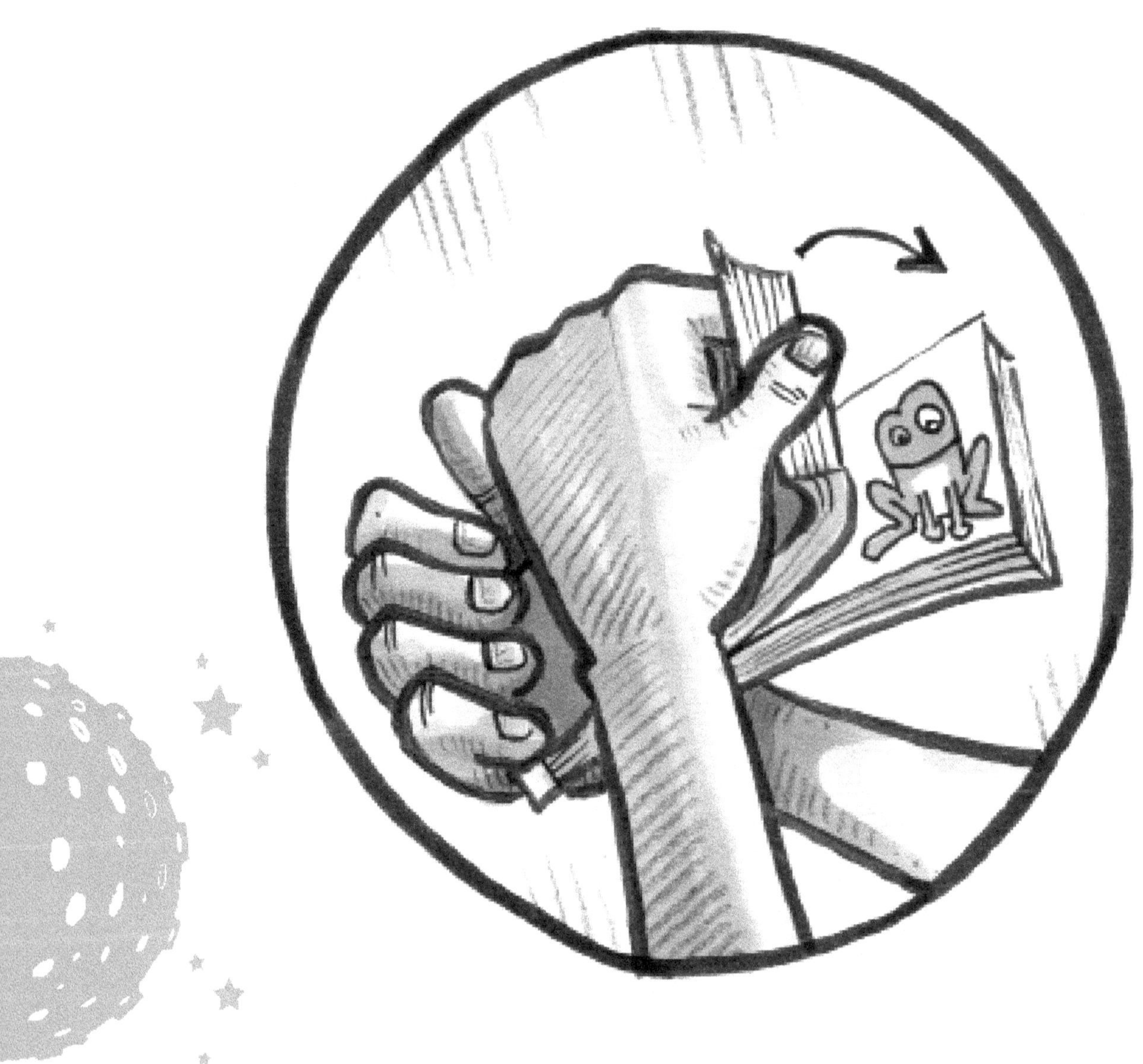

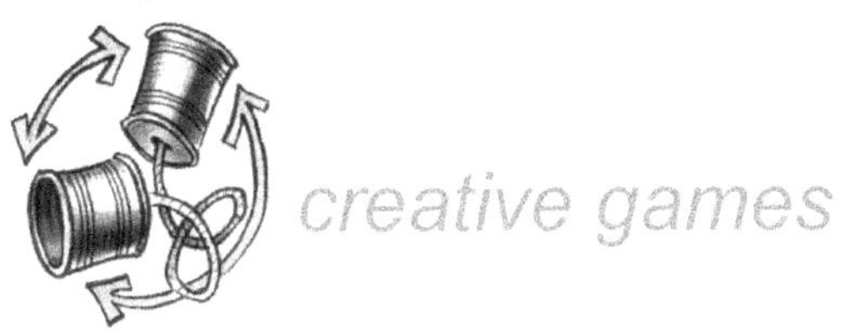

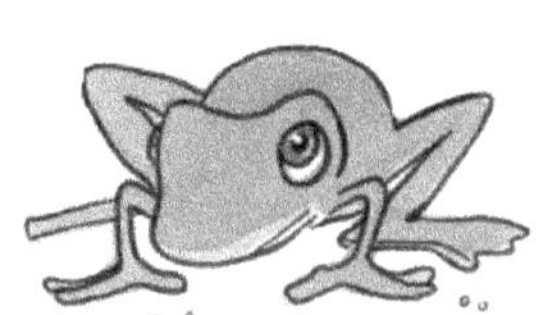

Beach Scribbles

Background: This is a game that is fun at the beach, but could also be played anywhere there is sand, mud or snow. It can be played with water on pavement. It is also fun to play with a piece of paper and a pen while waiting in a restaurant or at a bus stop.

The game involves taking a random scribble and adding lines to it to turn it into a drawing. It is best played with a friend, but you can even play alone if you don't think too much while you are making scribbles.

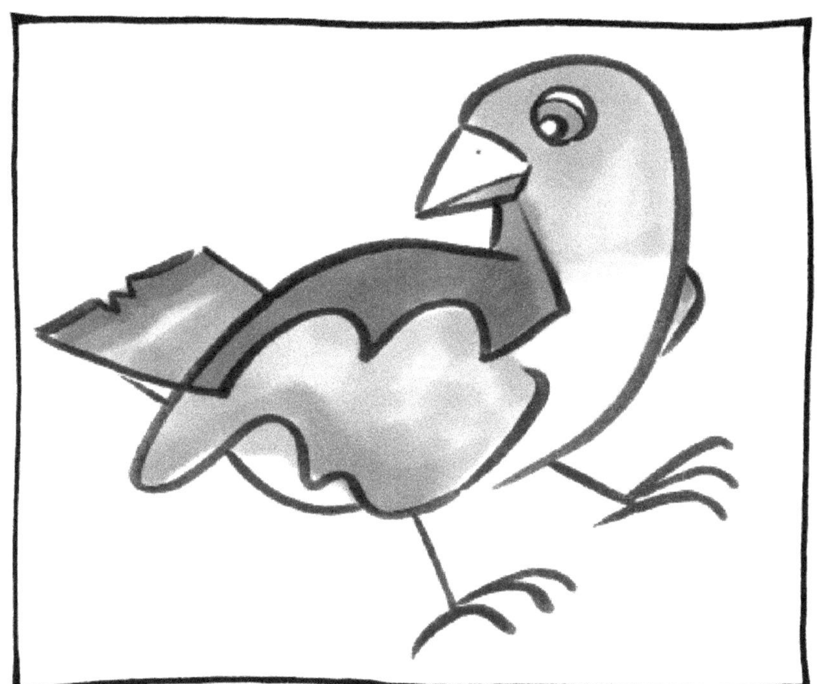

Materials: A beach, a friend, a stick.

Directions:

- One person starts the game by drawing a large, simple scribble on the sand. Perhaps it is a zigzag with a few little loops on the end.

- The other person takes the stick and adds marks to the scribble. They add a line here and a line there and suddenly, it looks like a mermaid.

- It is now the second person's turn to make a scribble for their friend. Their friend might turn it into a tyrannosaur.

- The friends continue playing the game down the beach until an entire gallery of giant drawings is created.

- The two friends sit in the sand and enjoy watching other beachgoers walking up the coast stop to enjoy the artwork.

Practice: To get you warmed up before you have a chance to go outside, try the scribbles on the next couple of pages. Remember that any direction can be up, so feel free to turn this book around.

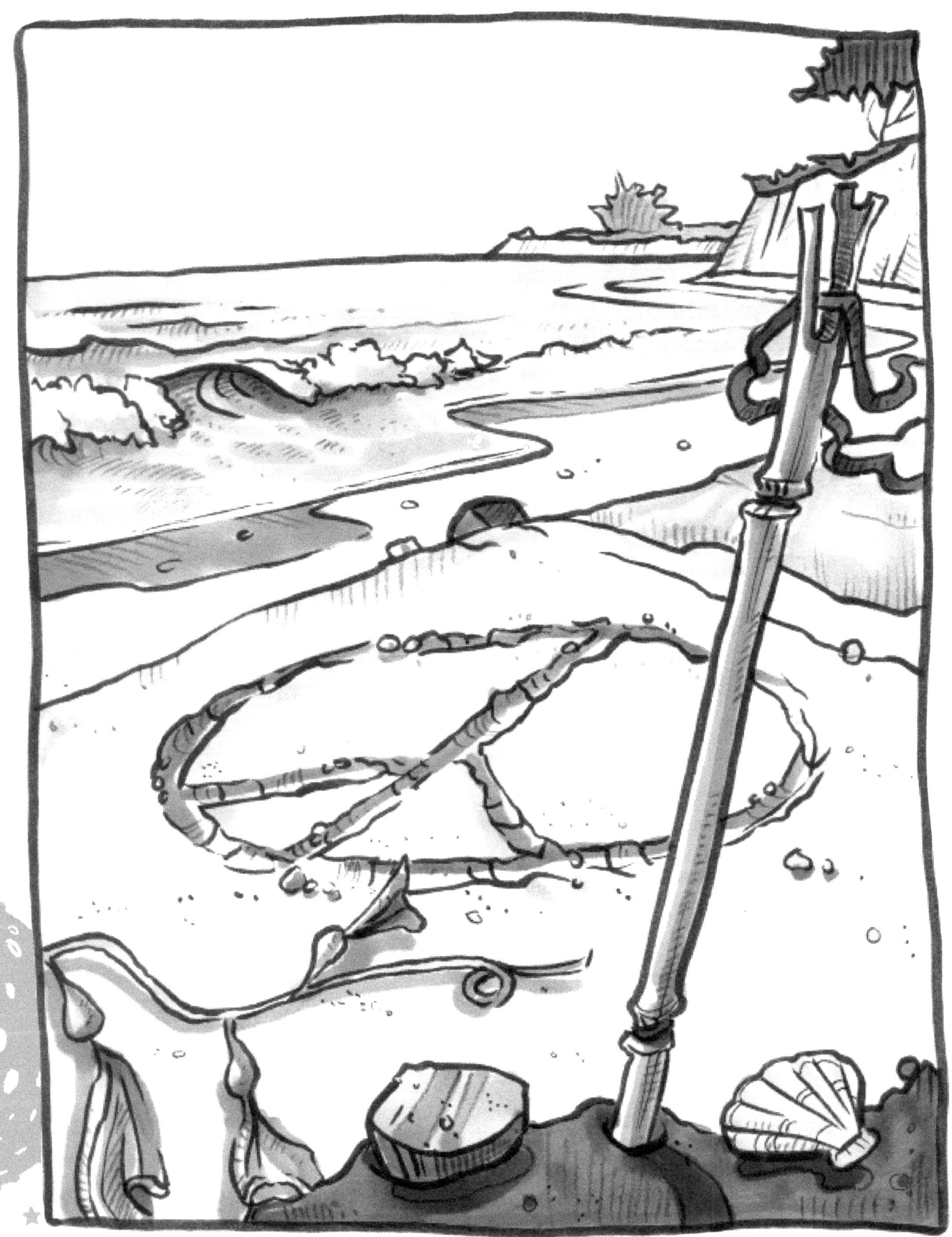

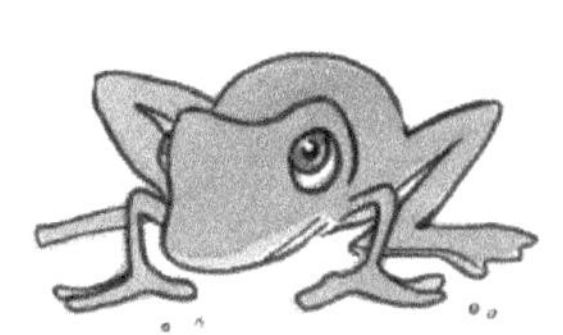

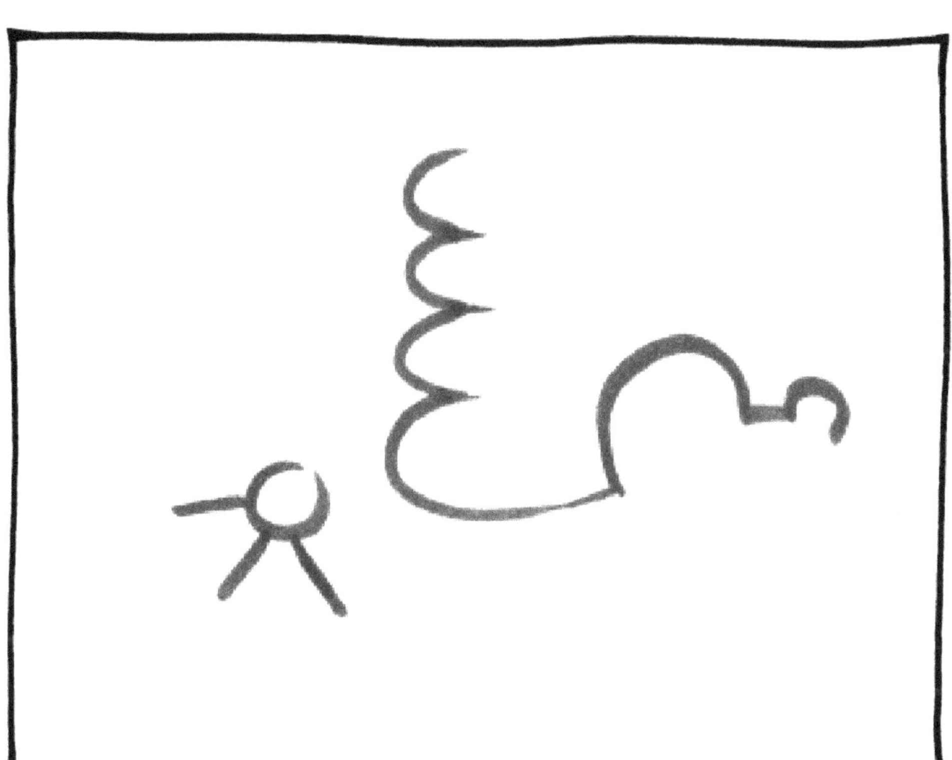

Can you turn these scribbles into images? Turn them in any direction. The bird on page 107 was drawn from the scribble below. Can you turn it into something completely different?

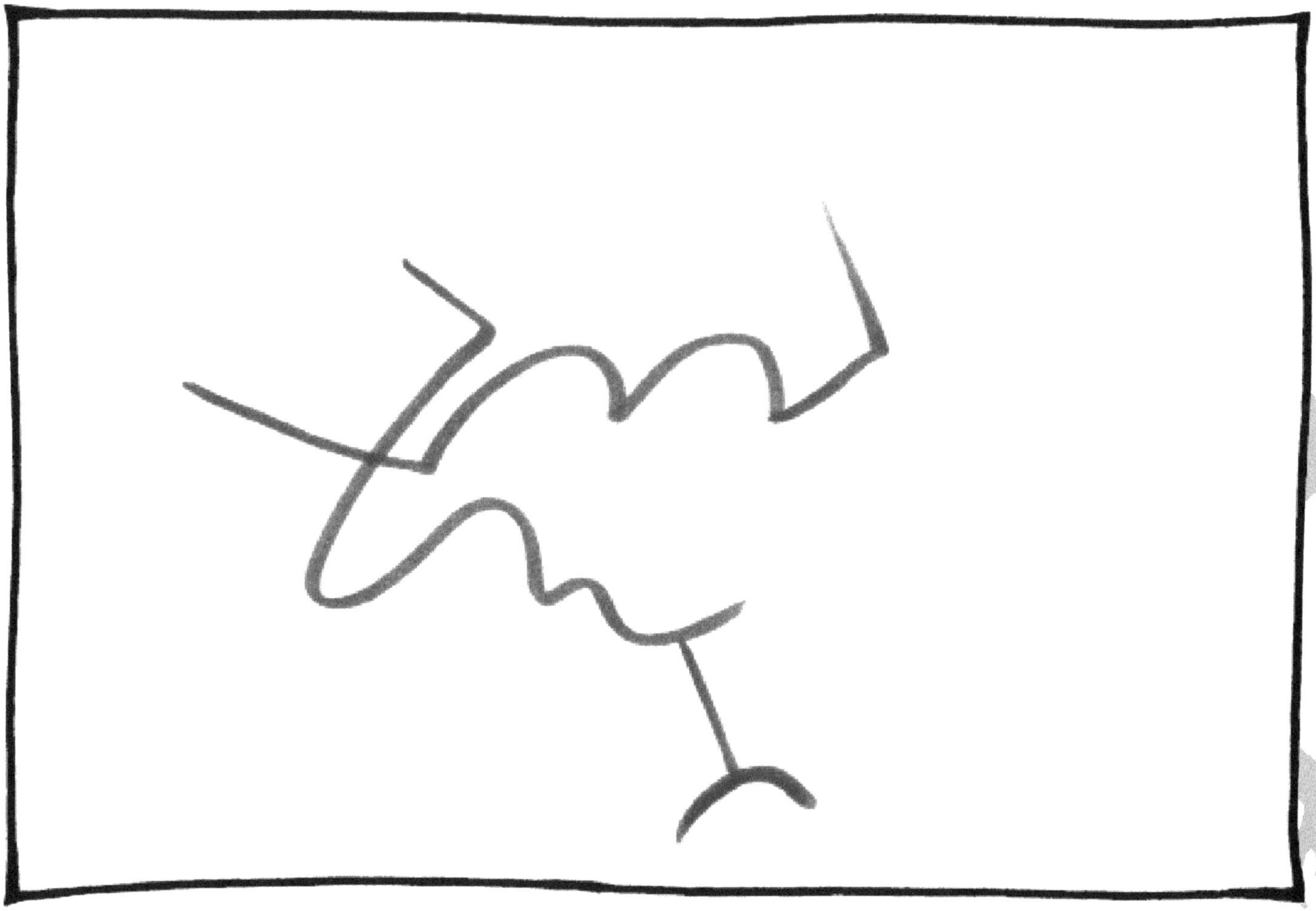

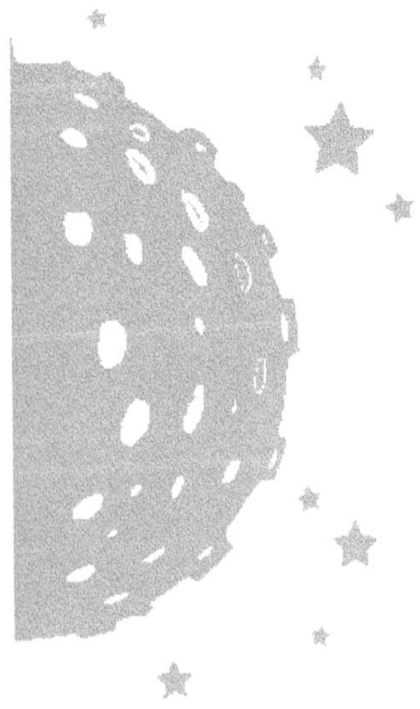